Making Youth Soccer Fun!

Ages 4 to 8

A Guide to Coaching

Paul Sabiston

Contents

Chapter 7

Chapter 8

Chapter 1

LET'S GET STARTED

INTRODUCTION

Making Youth Soccer Fun! will give any parent, volunteer, or a beginner in coaching all of the basic tools to teach and coach youth soccer players, both boys and girls, from ages 4 to approximately 8. Even former soccer players and experienced senior coaches will benefit from this book as it will provide them with a step-by-step guide, at the appropriate level, for what these young players need to improve in order to enjoy the great game of soccer.

If you are worried that you lack knowledge of soccer in general, its techniques, and the rules of the game; and do not know how to run a practice session or manage a team of 4-to-8-year-olds — fear no more! This book will help you with quick-and-easy-to-apply activities on the field as it provides straightforward answers to some critical soccer questions.

You do not need to be a former athlete or experienced coach in another sport — although that will not hurt you. For those of you that played or coached in another sport, even at a high level, this book will help you to convert your general sports knowledge into effective soccer coaching for beginning players.

WHAT THIS BOOK WILL PROVIDE

Making Youth Soccer Fun! will provide you with enough detailed practice plans and activities to get you through an entire season and more. It is easy to read and will explain in understandable terms how to teach kids basic soccer techniques while keeping the whole exercise at a fun level.

Where necessary, the information is divided into two segments: one is aimed at complete beginners (the ages of players Under 6 or "U6" players) while the other is meant for slightly more experienced 6-, 7-, or 8-year-olds (Under 8 or "U8" players). Finally, this book will help you to manage both your players *and* their parents at practice and during the games.

This book is not meant to complicate things. Do what you need to do as a coach and provide the basics that the players need in order to develop. If you learn nothing else during this season as a coach for young players, keep these fundamental principles in mind at all times:

1. Make both practices and games FUN and SIMPLE.

2. Be organized and go early to practices and games.

3. COMMUNICATE clearly with both players and parents.

4. Set a good example for them by being POSITIVE.

5. Keep the kids moving in various controlled activities (no "laps, lines or lectures") separated by short breaks (these activities are provided in this book for you).

6. At practice, focus on as much contact with the ball, or "touches", as possible through dribbling, shooting, or kicking the ball.

7. Give the players some "free play" with a ball at every practice — usually at the end.

You can read *Making Youth Soccer Fun!* in many different ways to suit your needs. Even if you do not read the book from beginning to end you can access it easily. It is organized into helpful chapters and you can jump to any one from the table of contents if you have a burning question or issue on that particular topic.

The chapters on practice plans, activities, drills and techniques assist you as a ready reference as you begin a practice session in any of these areas. If you are out of time following a busy day at work or home, just find one of the pre-designed practice activities on a topic of your choice and you are ready for that day's practice!

Kids having fun playing soccer!

Chapter 2

YOUTH SOCCER PHILOSOPHY & THE ROLE OF COACHES WITH BEGINNING SOCCER PLAYERS

Soccer at the ages of 4 to 8 can be most rewarding for player, parent and coach. The innocence of the game, players' lack of concern for results, and the "play" element of these early years are hard to find in older levels of soccer where both agony and ecstasy become present.

As the developmental needs and abilities of kids of this age group are limited, it is a coach's responsibility to train them within these limitations.

COACH'S RESTRAINT

As a coach for this age group, the first thing you must do is learn not to "over-coach" your young players. You should view yourself more as a team "helper" or "facilitator" than as a stereotypical coach.

This can be a difficult task for those of us that have played team sports at a high level. Kids in the age group of 4 to 8 are not expected to learn all the niceties of soccer - technically (individual skills) or tactically (team skills). You may be saying that is just fine because you do not know these details anyway. Well, consider yourself the perfect candidate to coach in this age group! Yes, the less you know about soccer may be the better for your players - within reason of course.

If you happen to have some basic soccer knowledge, or even more than that, you will simply have to place it on hold in many cases. Kids at this age need to focus on touching the ball by dribbling it and playing fun games that happen to involve, well, a soccer ball.

Trying to teach them how to play a position or how to pass the ball to an open space for a teammate to receive it would be mostly counterproductive at this stage. How is that possible, you may ask? Because if they cannot yet dribble the ball comfortably, the rest of the game has to wait.

Most of you have certainly seen how infants go from crawling to walking. It just happens. A parent might be around to hold his child upright by the hands, but you do not normally see the parent picking up the baby's legs and moving them alternately in a "walking motion." The baby's walking comes naturally.

> Mia Hamm, the Hall-of-Fame US Women's National Team Player, is credited with saying, "Failure happens all the time. It happens every day in practice. What makes you better is how you react."

Sometimes you need to just let soccer happen in the 4-8 age group. Some will learn to "walk," or in the case of soccer, dribble, faster and better than others. The slower ones will watch the others (or you) dribble a ball, learn it for themselves, and eventually DO IT. Let them fail, and then watch them succeed!

U6 AND U8 PLAYER CHARACTERISTICS - IT'S ALL ABOUT ME!

Generally speaking, players at ages 4, 5 and 6 (U6) have a short attention span, have little sophistication in their coordination, and they view everything from the perspective of how it will impact them personally – or "ME" from their point of view. There is little or no team concept. These limitations must be taken into account when creating practice activities.

On the other hand, while the fitness endurance for U6 players is limited, when they do play they go all out for short periods of time. They enjoy running, jumping, rolling and playing games. Also, while their attention span is short, they do respond well to simple, short instructions. They can be very creative, like to play "pretend" games, and can also be extremely focused on a single task even if for only a short time. All of these attributes must be taken advantage of as a coach for this age group.

At the ages of 6 to 8 (U8), while still inconsistent, their attention spans are increasing and they are able to focus on a single task or activity for longer periods. U8 players are typically talkative and while still creative and imaginative, they also like to learn from repetition. You will notice a stronger sense of independence in them, but they still thrive on praise and positive reinforcement from their coach.

On the physical side, the U8 player is exploding with new found coordination and athletic ability. At this stage, balance and the ability to display more finely tuned motor skills such as dribbling, develop rapidly. Coaches should still rely heavily on the visual demonstration technique for teaching; but these U8 players are starting to visualize and verbalize soccer lessons.

If you continue to coach for a few years, you will often hear the phrase "the game is the best teacher." While being true, it holds different meanings for different ages. In the U6 and U8 age groups, young players are not meant to start learning how to play a "game" like the adult players you see on the TV or even like those in the U12 or U14 age groups. That comes later - much later.

At this introductory age, the "game" is simply dribbling the ball around as well as possible, playing some offense where the ball is kicked into a goal, and playing some defense by trying to take the ball away from the other team. That is all, but then that is plenty to work on for the first season or two of soccer. You will have plenty to do if you can handle it properly.

MENTAL, PHYSICAL AND SOCIAL DEVELOPMENT

In summary, the levels of development — mentally, physically and emotionally/socially — for **U6 players** are as follows:

U6s

Mental: Creative, strong imagination, short attention span but focused, repetition-based learning
Visual learning by short, simple demonstrations

Physical: Short endurance, all-out effort in short bursts
Big muscles in play - running, jumping, rolling
Beginning coordination and balance

Emotional/Social: Easily led, want to please, like to be praised and supported
Can be frustrated quickly, if not encouraged
Display independent learning habits

For the **U8 players** add these to the list:

U8s

Mental: Greater concentration for longer periods, keen on experiments
More verbal communication, quickly developing learning abilities

Physical: Better endurance, much-improved coordination
Big muscles very much at work - running, jumping, rolling, etc.

Finely tuned motor skills rapidly improving now

Emotional/Social: Social skills developing now, still like to be praised and supported

Greater independence in solving problems

Learn by physical repetition — more so now than in the U6 age group

U6 AND U8 COACHING CHARACTERISTICS - THE GOOD, THE BAD, AND THE UGLY!

Just to get you started in the right direction, I want to give you a few basic principles to think about as you read the rest of this book. These rules, split into "The Good" (try to follow), "The Bad" (try to avoid), and "The Ugly" (definitely avoid), deal with everything from coaching attitude to practice details and will be touched on throughout this book.

The Good (Try to Follow):

- Make it Fun!
- Keep it simple
- Keep it relatively short
- Make it safe
- Be positive and friendly
- Be early
- Be organized but flexible
- Be supportive and praise frequently
- Tell them what "to do" instead of what "not to do"
- Keep things moving at a good pace
- "Play" more and "coach" less
- Demonstrate (skills) more and talk less
- Insure maximum contact with ball ("touches")
- Teach by playing games
- 1 v. 1 and 2 v. 2 games

- Take frequent but short breaks
- Provide for "free play"
- Repeat *everything* as needed
- Communicate clearly with parents

The Bad (Try to Avoid):

- Late and unprepared
- Laps - for fitness or punishment
- Lines – making them wait in lines to do something
- Lectures - they won't listen and these are boring
- Using advanced words or phrases
- Teaching advanced skills beyond dribbling and kicking
- Teaching any "tactics" except maybe which way to go
- Teaching "positions"

The Ugly (Definitely Avoid):

- Impatience
- Loud voice in a negative tone
- Keeping score or worrying about results
- And yes, stupid outfits that make you look unprofessional or scary

The lists above attempt to give you some sense of "right and wrong" about coaching topics, methods and mannerisms. These are the fundamental elements of coaching young beginners. Remember that improving the individual players on your team is more important at these ages than strengthening your "team" as a whole. Again, that will come later.

This is where you really have to know your players **individually** and try to coach them somewhat individually to their strengths and improve their weaknesses. Small groups of players and activities that use 1 v. 1 (where one player faces another) and 2 v. 2 (two players taking on another two) are crucial at this stage of development.

Chapter 3

THE BASICS

Let's get started with what you need to know to kick off your season. In this chapter you will get an idea about the basic tools and structure you need to begin your season with. It also enlightens you on equipment needs, team management essentials, and some basic soccer terminology. You should be familiar with these terms so that you can understand what other more experienced coaches or parents might be discussing. It will help you to introduce these terms to your players when appropriate.

EQUIPMENT

We have discussed briefly the philosophical approach to coaching young soccer players from ages 4 to 8 in Chapter 1. We will continue with this topic in much more detail in the following chapters; but now let's look at something more concrete. What "stuff" do you need to create a good learning environment for the players during your practice sessions?

The equipment on the first list below should be considered the "must have/bare essentials." The second list includes extra items that would be "nice to have" if you could borrow or afford to buy them.

This book receives no benefit from retailers or Web sites when we make referrals - this is simply practical advice. Most of the items listed below can be found new at wholesale/retail online stores such as www.soccer.com, www.worldsoccershop.com, and www.amazon.com. There are also Web sites that specialize in used items such as your local www.craigslist.org and www.eBay.com.

Also, do not forget your local sporting goods stores. Your fellow coaches can be useful too. They may be looking to replace some of their older equipment with something more appropriate for older players as they move up the coaching chain. Most coaches are generous enough to help out a newer coach in a younger age group. Finally, many soccer associations will provide you with basic equipment at their own expense to help you get started - so ask.

Must Have/Essential Equipment:

1. **Soccer balls.** You need four or five of them of Size 3. However, each player should bring his/her own Size 3 ball to practice sessions. The size is printed on the ball. Also, look for balls that indicate some form of "official" approval. Try to find light, highly waterproof balls. The ones that feel "sticky" are usually the best for these age groups. Expect to spend US $10-$20 per ball if purchased new.

2. **Plastic disc cones.** These are low, flat cones with a hole in the middle. Buy 40+ orange, yellow, red or blue disc cones; but try to have a basic color, such as orange, and get at least 20 cones of that color.

   Write your name or initials on each cone with a black permanent marker. If the cones do not come with a belt or stick tie, which smoothly threads through them and ties them together for storage, get a short bungie cord or nylon clip belt to do the job. Cones will cost you $0.30-$0.50 per cone.

3. **Training/scrimmage vests.** Get two sets of six of two different colors. These are colorful pullover vests, sometimes called "pinnies" or "bibs," used by players of all ages to divide teams for various activities or scrimmages. The vests are typically mesh and come in bright colors like green, yellow, red and blue. Get youth sizes ranging from small to medium.

Having enough vests to allow your team to be divided into two playing units is a great benefit. If you can swing it, a third set of six vests, yet another color, is nice to have. Expect to spend about $20 for a set of six.

4. **Large mesh soccer bag.** This is how you will carry all of your basic equipment and balls. Expect to be poorer by $8-$15.

5. **Personal items for the coach.** A whistle, a watch or a cell phone with watch/timer, appropriate shorts/training pants with pockets, comfortable shirt and shoes (the soccer turf variety makes great coaching shoes that work well on almost all surfaces and still provide decent traction), a hat, and sunscreen. Costs will vary.

Some basic equipment that you need to coach: balls, ball bag, various cones, different-colored pinnies, whistle,

watch and even some training poles.

Extra Gear that Comes in Handy:

1. **Upright cones or large disc cones.** These are the more traditional cones that stand about 10 to 12 inches high, of a triangular shape, or are raised five or six inches off the ground if they are large "disc" cones. The more distinct triangular cones are nice to have, in addition to the circular and relatively flat ones, for use as corner markers, dribbling obstacles, and targets.

2. **Two small pop-up portable goals.** Two examples are Pugg and Kwik Goal, their products are provided in either four or six feet in width. These "pop-up goals" are easy to find in the market. They can be expensive, at $40 to $60 each, but are extremely useful.

   These goals literally pop up when untied and provide a nice, small, portable goal to be used for countless drills and basic scrimmage activities. They are typically shaped like an upside down "U" and are made of mesh netting with a flexible rod sewn into the edge. They come with small stakes for securing them to the ground.

3. **A set of six 6-foot-tall poles.** Staked into the ground, these poles can be used as temporary goals, obstacles to weave through, corner sticks, etc. They are simply spiked poles; sometimes they break down into two sections of equal length for ease of transporting. A set of six costs about $60.

4. **Portable, collapsible benches and a canopy tent.** Having a couple of benches that seat four to six players and a 10-by-10 foot canopy tent will keep you and your players out of the sun during games. The benches range from $70 to $140 each and the canopy from $70 to $120 depending on quality.

5. **Clipboard or dry-erase board.** Procure one to keep notes

and to diagram the basics for the players when needed. You will spend $12-$18 based on size.

Above shows you some basic equipment for you the coach – everything from a hat, dry-erase board to sunglasses, sunscreen, and "slides" to wear in the car.

What Do the Players Need?

1. **Shin guards.** Buy the ones that come with ankle pads/heel stirrups for greater protection. Shin guards are a *no-exception-and-must-have* piece of equipment that each player needs at every practice and game. It is recommended that the coach keep an extra pair of the "tuck in" type so that he/she can come to the rescue of a forgetful player when needed.

2. **Ball.** Get a Size 3.

3. **Cleats or athletic shoes**. Cleats are nice but not absolutely necessary at the U6 level. A pair of solid tennis/gym shoes with some tread will work just fine at this stage. At U8, a pair of affordable cleats is the best option as kids start to cut and run with more power at this age.

4. **Water bottle.** Plastic type, with easily removable cap/lid, and with a capacity of at least 16 ounces, and 32 ounces is better. Have the parents write the player's name or initials on it and all other equipment belonging to their child!

5. **Soccer socks.** Make sure they reach the knees. Proper socks will make your team look like soccer players. Also, these socks hold the player's shin guards in place; and they protect him/her from receiving abrasions from poorly covered shin guards of others.

Player equipment must include a water jug, shoes, either cleats or "flats" or turf shoes, shin guards, long socks and a ball – size 3.

TEAM MANAGEMENT

We have discussed some basic coaching philosophy and equipment needs for you, your players and your team. Now, let's focus on the management of your team's affairs before, during, and at the end of the season. This section will show you how to manage players and parents off the field and between practice sessions and games.

Team management is similar to running a small social club

or even a small business in some respects. Think of the players' parents as your clients and you are in the business of providing a service to these clients, namely, coaching and introducing sports, specifically soccer, into the lives of their children.

Your success or failure will be largely judged on whether or not the players *and their parents* are happy with your efforts during the season. Although a few parents may miss the big picture, the season should not be judged on wins and losses at the U6 or U8 age levels. So do not bother yourself about the results.

As discussed in Chapter 1, at this age of development you have three primary goals. The first is to introduce the game of soccer at a fundamental level. The second is to teach the players a few basic activities that involve dribbling, kicking, some defense, and improving their athleticism, such as running, moving, and jumping. For some, possibly some short passing and ball control. Finally, the most important element is to create a fun environment for your players with the sport of soccer at the center of that enjoyment. *Always keep these basics foremost in your coaching efforts at this level!*

So, once you are assigned a team and given a roster, I strongly urge you to introduce yourself to the parents as soon as possible and to schedule the first team meeting and/or practice. A short team meeting before the first practice is a good way to get started.

You should allow and take only about 20 to 30 minutes for the team/parent meeting if it is before a practice session. The players may attend most, if not all, of the meeting. **Pro Tip 1:** Communicate often and clearly with the parents.

At the meeting, you need to do the following:

1. Introduce yourself and speak to each parent and player.

2. Give the parents the practice schedule and, if available, the game schedule for the season too.

3. Request the parents to complete carefully a "contact form" (with name, address, telephone numbers, emails, etc.) and any additional forms, such as a medical waiver, if needed by your association. They can do this during the practice session and you can collect those forms at the end of the session.

4. Find two key parent volunteers - a) a contact coordinator and b) a snack/team party coordinator.

5. Establish how you (or the contact coordinator) will communicate with the parents - text, email, telephone, etc.

6. Define your role as coach for this age group by explaining what you are going to do — introducing your players to a few basic skills and rules of the game, focusing on basic skills development and, hopefully, creating some improvement in the players' athleticism. Equally important should be your effort to make the sport enjoyable for the young players.

   Pro Tip 2: Ask the parents to help you by staying positive — at home and on the sidelines — about their kids' performance and not judge it solely on winning or losing games. The emphasis should be on improving and having fun.

Practice and Game Schedules. If you have to seek or schedule a practice session or two each week with your league or association (and this will vary from association to association and among age groups), do so as early as possible. **Pro Tip 3:** You are the coach and you are volunteering your time, so make your practice times/days relatively convenient for your schedule as much as reasonably possible. Be fair but be smart - you are the one that has to get to practice early, set up the equipment, and be prepared.

If you have the game schedule go ahead and distribute it at the meeting. If you do not, let the parents know what to expect in general, such as "We play our games on Saturday mornings usually between 8am and 12 noon and I will distribute the schedule as soon as I have it." Some leagues may not let this age group play games at all - and that is totally acceptable. Such non-game leagues typically offer a weekly scrimmage without keeping score and simply encourage fun with a soccer ball. Just go with it - it is a good idea for positive development without pressure and the kids will thoroughly enjoy themselves.

Paperwork

Forms. Once you have set up the date and time for the team meeting, you should prepare a few forms that will help you throughout the season. The first one is a basic contact form that will seek full names, addresses, cell phone numbers, best cell numbers to text, email addresses, emergency contacts, special needs, etc., of the players' parents.

Make sure the parents complete this form in full and in clear handwriting. On occasion, parents will forget to pick up a player or simply get caught in traffic. I cannot tell you how many times I have had to go through these forms to ferret out a parent's contact number in an emergency or when a player is waiting for a ride home after a practice or game.

More Forms. Other forms, such as that for a medical waiver, are typically required but may already be filled out as part of the registration process with your association. You should verify this process with your association's Director of Coaching if you are unsure. Most times the associations request the coaches to get this form filled out before practices begin, in which case you should not allow players to participate until this form is completed and signed by their parents or guardians.

At the U8 and older ages, I would recommend that you obtain a copy of each player's birth certificate for your file. These can come in handy when registering for certain tournaments that you may choose to enter later in the season. The association may (and should) have a copy of a birth certificate but, trust me, it is much easier if you have your own copy at the U8 and older age levels.

Assistance and Communication

Team Coordinators. Next, the two parent volunteers chosen at the meeting as contact coordinator and snack/party coordinator are important members of your "management team."

The contact coordinator will insure that all messages regarding practices, games, weather cancellations, announcements, etc. are timely delivered to all team parents. The snack coordinator will equally sign up all parents to bring (or share in bringing) an appropriate snack for game days. **Pro Tip 4:** If you can find effective coordinators, your job just became much easier for the season; so seek good parent volunteers as your coordinators!

How to Communicate with Your Team. At the team meeting you must explain to the parents how you (or your coordinator) will communicate with them. In this age of information where the Internet has witnessed a massive explosion of electronic messaging systems and social media sites, information sharing has become much easier than it used to be. Most teams these days will use either text messaging or email to communicate basic messages and changes to a schedule.

Some associations will have accessible Web pages for your own team where you can post messages. I have seen that some teams, for whatever reason, are more responsive to text messaging than to email or vice-versa. Find out at the team meeting which method of communication works best for your team, and then test them both out and use both for important messages. Try not to have different types of messaging for several groups of parents — a cell phone group, a text only group, and then an email only group. It is simply too much trouble. Private commercial text/email systems, such as www.teamsnap.com, are available and extremely affordable for contact systems.

Calling always works for most parents but it is the most time-consuming method. Save it for emergencies. I prefer to text and/or email key schedule changes or messages because it is quick and easy. Help your team contact coordinator to work through this early on during the season and then let him or her handle it.

As the coach, however, always make sure you have an active and accurate contact list so that you are able to make contacts directly without having to go through a coordinator if and when you need to do so. Never completely relinquish that ability and, on occasions, be sure to send out a "good job" to the parents of your players after a good practice or game effort - even if you "lost." **Pro Tip 5:** Send out a good positive team text or email at least once every 10 days — the earlier, the better — about how the team is progressing or improving; or you might say, "We all need to be patient" if things are moving slowly. For example, "Good practice last night, the team is improving on its dribbling skills. See you at the game this Sat. at 10am at Smith Park Field 2A."

Positive Role Model. As a coach for a team of beginners, your influence on the players will be the most significant for their young careers. Your role is not necessarily to make them the most skillful and talented players at the age of 5 or 6; that can come later. As a coach you should get them started in the right direction.

If you remain positive and the players are having fun, the

drills and activities that are included in this book will give you the tools that will help them immensely to improve on the field. **Pro Tip 6:** Be a positive role model for your players and parents both on and off the field.

Other Team Management Items

Get a Notebook Binder with a Zipper. These zip-up, three-ring binders made of synthetic fabric are great to put all your player contact forms in. You can also store medical information, your schedule, practice plans, whistles, etc., in it. Place several three-hole punched plastic sleeves (one for each player plus a few more) into the binder and simply slide all of your paperwork into those sleeves as needed. If your league uses/requires individual "player cards" for your team, this is a great place to file away those cards too.

You May Need an Assistant Coach. Find and draft an assistant coach if you can. It is amazing how much another adult can assist you with the handling of 7 to 12 kids at a practice or game. **Pro Tip 7:** During practice sessions, having an assistant setting up the next activity, while you finish the present one, saves both time and energy.

During a game event, an assistant can help make sure that you have played all players at least half the game and that the bench players are behaving. Make sure that your association allows for an assistant coach and that he or she meets all requirements for participation. Most associations require some sort of background check for all coaches and team managers.

Parents Who Do Not Help. You will have some parents that use the team as a baby-sitting service and simply do not assist in any manner. If you and others have tried unsuccessfully to engage them, then simply work around them. You cannot fix all things and all people but be sure to be inclusive and encourage their children as much as you do others — these children should not pay for their parents' lack of interest in their activities.

Parents Who Help Too Much. This is a good problem to have and you need to give them something to do. If the coordinator roles are already filled, maybe these parents can assist one of them with his/her duties. Or you can create a special job for them, like keeping "stats" during a game for the number of successful passes per game per player, number of shots per game, etc. If not a coach, let them chase balls (if they are allowed on the field by your association) during practice or game warm-ups. **Pro Tip 8:** For the sake of soccer keep these parents busy!

Year-End Team Party. Organize a fun party at the end of the season. Your snack/team party coordinator can arrange this with your guidance. Whether you go to a kid-friendly restaurant/facility or simply have a picnic or small gathering following your last game, it should be a fun social event for the players. It does not need to be expensive or time consuming but simple with lots of fun for the kids.

I am not a "give a trophy to every player just for showing up" kind of coach, but if your league follows that path then this year-end event is a great time to hand out the hardware and make a positive, encouraging statement about each player. Using basic computer software we have created our own team "certificates" with nicknames for players such as "Captain Speed" or "Mr. Big Shot" to highlight their individual qualities. They love it! Try to make a few positive remarks about each player — they all have something special.

Soccer Terms

Here are a few terms and definitions from the soccer world

to help you talk the language and understand what others are discussing. Many of these terms are from Great Britain and reflect its usage and forms of expression.

Activity. Any practice session event where the players work together, with or without a ball, to learn a skill, technique, and, when older, a tactic. It also includes simple exercises like running or jumping at the younger ages and, again, when older, fitness training. Soccer does not like the term "drill" — sounds too much like work!

Boots. A general term for soccer shoes or cleats.

Chip. Kicking the ball so that it rises quickly and softly into the air. It is usually done to beat a defender by placing the ball behind him/her or to serve a pass to a teammate or the space behind a defender.

Cross or Center. When the ball is delivered from the side or flanks of the field into the middle or "center" of the field — typically in the mouth of the goal to create a goal-scoring opportunity.

Dead ball. This is when the ball has gone out of play and may be handled by the team that will take the resulting throw-in, corner kick, kick-off, goal kick or free kick.

EPL. "English Premier League" which is the highest division of men's professional soccer/football league in England. Teams such as Arsenal, Chelsea, Liverpool and Manchester United are long-time members of this league.

Fake or Feint. A move, or cut, or change of speed by one player meant to deceive one or more opponents. It may occur when dribbling, passing or shooting.

Far post. It is the goal post that is farthest away from a player who is running down either side of the playing field with or without a ball. Thus, if you are on the right side of the field, the "far post" for you is the goal post on the left side of the goal that you face. When a coach says "far post" he means the space in front of that post as he suggests a pass or cross, and the space just inside of the post when suggesting a shot on goal. The "near post" is the goal post closest to the player.

First time. A player passes, kicks, volleys or heads a ball with only a single touch to another player, on goal or to clear the ball out of danger. It is an advanced skill but an essential one for older players.

Free kick. The team that has been fouled is awarded a kick of a non-moving ball from the place of the foul and the fouling team must remain 8 to 10 yards (depending on age group) away from the ball. In some cases, depending on the type of foul committed, the ball may be allowed to be kicked directly into the goal (direct kicks) and, in the other cases, it must be touched by another player before it is kicked into the goal (indirect kicks).

Goalmouth. It is the general area in front of the goal and is not precisely marked with lines. It is simply a term which is used to give players a general guideline on where to collect a loose ball to either score a goal, as a striker playing in the opponent's zone, or clear it away as a defender. Anything within roughly 3 to 6 yards of a small U6/U8 goal, and 3 to 10 yards for older levels, would be considered the "goalmouth".

Half-volley. This is a kicking action where a player kicks the ball immediately after it bounces off the ground (as opposed to a volley where one kicks an incoming ball directly out of the air, before it hits the ground).

Hat trick. When a player scores at least three goals in a single match.

Header. Players use their heads to redirect the ball. The forehead is the proper surface to use for headers and not the top of the head.

Instep. The top arched portion of your foot which is closer to your ankle as far as soccer is concerned. It is a great place to make contact with the middle of the ball for a strong shot.

Juggling. Where a player continuously touches the ball with his foot, thigh, head or other parts of his body (but not the hands or arms) to keep a soccer ball bouncing into the air under his control and without hitting the ground. It is a great practice exercise.

La Liga. It is the highest division of men's professional soccer/football in Spain. Teams such as Barcelona and Real Madrid are famous members of this league.

Linesman. This is an assistant referee who stays on the sideline with a flag to help the referee in the center of the field with offsides, out-of-bounds balls, and general fouls in his area during a game. There are usually two linesmen, one for each sideline, at the older levels of soccer. Usually, there are no linesmen for U6 and U8 soccer games — the referee (center official) handles all calls.

Mark. When a player covers or stays with an opponent to prevent that player from receiving or advancing the ball. It is "man-to-man" marking in that case. Now if that player guards a general area of the field and defends any opponents when entering it, this becomes "zonal" or "zone" marking.

MLS. Major League Soccer is the highest division of men's professional soccer in the United States. Teams such as DC United and the LA Galaxy are long-time members of this league.

NWSL. National Women's Soccer League is the highest division of women's professional soccer in the United States. The Seattle Reign FC and Chicago Red Stars are members of this league.

One touch. See "First time" above.

Own goal. When a player inadvertently passes a ball, or it is deflected off him, into his "own goal" the resulting score counts for the other team. It happens so don't worry too much about it.

Pitch. Soccer lingo for the playing field or game field.

Possession. A situation in which a team is in control of the ball with its players passing it to one another (team possession) or a player is in possession of it when dribbling alone(individual possession).

Push pass. A simple pass made with the inside of the foot, held in the position of an "L," by pushing the ball on the ground toward an intended target. Sometimes it is used to shoot the ball on goal too.

Re-start. When a game is stopped for a foul; the ball goes out of bounds for a throw-in; there is a goal kick; or a kick-off takes place after a goal is scored; it is "re-started" by various methods. Also, a part of the game is called a "set piece" when a re-start presents a goal-scoring opportunity since the flight of the ball and movements of the players are planned and coordinated.

Save. The goalkeeper catches, deflects, or kicks away an incoming ball thus preventing a goal from being scored.

Side. This is merely either of the two playing teams.

Slide tackle. A player slides along the ground on his side in an effort to kick the ball away from an opposing player in possession of it. The ball must be won cleanly and contacted first before any contact is made with the opposing player. It is not really necessary or encouraged in the early years of soccer. Usually, it is not allowed till the players are old enough for it because it can be dangerous.

Tackle. Where a defending player takes the ball away with his foot from another player possessing it. This is usually accomplished by kicking the ball away or winning it with the inside or outside of the foot.

Touchline. It is one of the sidelines of a soccer field. Unlike in most other sports, if the ball touches the line it is still in bounds. It must go completely over the sideline or endline to be out of bounds.

Volley. It is a kicking action where a player kicks a ball which is in flight usually at the knee level or higher (instead of kicking it immediately after it bounces off the ground as in a half-volley).

Chapter 4

PRACTICE SESSIONS - SIMPLE AND ORGANIZED

Now that we have reviewed the basics of coaching philosophy and the other important aspects of soccer, let's get into the essence of a soccer program - the weekly practice sessions. Here, we will focus more on the structure or set-up of a practice session and less on the qualities of the coach or coaching techniques.

This chapter will show you a simple structure of a practice session that can be used repeatedly. All you will need to do is choose from the individual activities (offered later in Chapters 5 and 6) and plug them into the practice session structure for fun and effective practices each week.

SIMPLE AND ORGANIZED

You have already heard several times the need to be both simple and organized in dealing with these kindergartners to 3rd graders looking to you for a good start in soccer. Here are the basic structural elements that apply to *practice sessions* at the U6 and U8 age levels:

- Length of time - 35 to 45 minutes (U6) and 45 to 60 minutes (U8).

- One ball per player - Size 3 if available.

- Three to four short activities at each session separated by three-to-four-minute water breaks.

- Use individual and "small-sided" activities. Divide a team of 6 to 10 players into smaller groups for certain activities if you have assistant coaches to help out; if not, do the best you can.

- Use "active" rest periods between repetitions during an activity - that is, players touching a ball and moving it with their feet instead of just standing and waiting for their next turn.

- **Pro Tip 9:** Always have about 10 to 15 minutes — or longer — of "free play" at every practice session. This is where the kids play "Keep Away" or actually "scrimmage" to score goals without much or any coaching.

This is one of the few age groups that let parents participate on occasions in a practice session. The idea is to show the parents a few games/activities that they can take home along with their kids for the benefit of the latter. This time spent is not really "coaching" or "assisting" but more of a "how to" session going from you to the parents. (You should still check this out with your association to make sure that it is all right for them to help and that they do not need to complete a background check or other documents in order to participate in this manner.)

PRACTICE FORMAT

The practice session for U6/U8 players should be organized as follows:

1. Warm-up Activity or Game (10 to 12 minutes)

   Short Water Break (2 minutes)

2. Small-sided Activity and/or Individual Ball Skills (15 to 18 minutes)

   Short Water Break (3 to 4 minutes)

3. Team Activity/Free Play (10 to 15 minutes)

   This format will allow you the freedom to work on a variety

of activities and to adjust your practice schedule to fit the needs of your *players*. Notice I did not say "to fit the needs of your *team*." That is because the "team" element is not really important at these age levels and, therefore, you do not need to be pre-occupied with trying to create a "great team" tactically or otherwise.

While the individual concepts of getting along, mutual respect among players and for the coach, and helping your teammates can be introduced, the idea of team soccer is secondary at this age. Focus on improving the individual skills — primarily dribbling — of your players. That is the most important function for you as the coach of U6/U8 players.

Where possible, try to incorporate a "theme" into your entire practice session. For instance, the day's theme could be "keeping the ball close while dribbling" or "short passing" for more advanced players. For that session try to find activities that foster this concept for your players. It is your job as coach to emphasize the topic for your players. At this age use only one main topic to keep the players focused.

Warm-Up Activity / Games - Setting the Tone

This is the first part of practice and the first "activity" of the session. As mentioned in the "soccer terms" portion of Chapter 3, an "activity" is any practice session event where the players work together, with or without a ball, to learn a skill, technique and, when older, a tactic. It also includes simple exercises like running or jumping for younger players and fitness training for the older ones.

Modern soccer tends to frown on practice events being referred to as "drills" because of the negative connotations of that term. The idea is that "activities" should in most cases be more than mindless repetition of the same movements (i.e., drills). The players should have to think their ways through some aspects of it.

So, this first activity should set a positive and fun tone for the practice session. Hopefully this positive tone will ring through the entire practice and you can teach the players a few things while they are in a good frame of mind and receptive to learning. The fun tone, the key to the first activity, lets the kids enjoy the basic freedom to run and play and/or jump and just move for a few minutes without too many rules or "skill requirements" getting in their way.

I like to divide the "Warm-up" phase of practice into two parts. The first is a basic game that may or may not involve a ball and the second part — very easy and fun-based — involves a ball. For the first part, play simple child games (and there are some examples in Chapter 6) such as the old classic "tag," freeze tag, freezbee toss, kick a beach ball and chase it, Simon Says, Capture the Flag (short version), play Team Keep Away by throwing an American football/rugby ball, or any similar childhood games that you remember and that young kids like to play.

Here is a key to all of the diagrams:

Key to Diagrams

Below is an example of two such games:

Diagram 1 – Tag

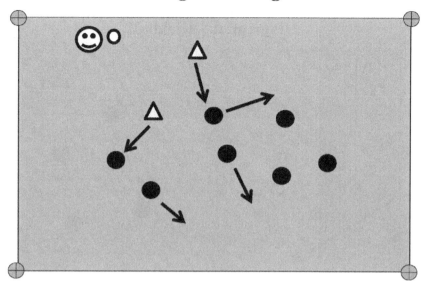

Set-Up: Find an open area approximately 20 x 30 yards in size. Cones are not necessary unless you think you need them. Place two players in the same colored pinnies

Game: This is a warm-up game and simply involves playing the classic game of tag and/or freeze tag if your kids like that one better. No ball is needed. The two players ("it") wearing pinnies seek out all other players and try to tag them. Once tagged a player becomes "it" and the old "it" player hands over the pinnie to the new one and runs away from her. If you play "freeze tag" you need the same set-up as above but once a player is tagged she must "freeze" in place and the two tagging players seek out the remaining players until all are tagged and frozen.

Coaching Points: This is simply a fun warm-up for the players to do and it does not require soccer skills at all. It develops basic athleticism of the players as they run, cut and dodge one another. Make the space smaller (with cones) if the tagging players are struggling.

Adjustments: This is a good practice starter to help set the tone for the remainder of a session. Another version of this classic game is that once a player is "tagged" she is added to the number of "taggers" and you keep tagging new players and adding them until the last player remains – who is the winner.

Diagram 2 – Kickball

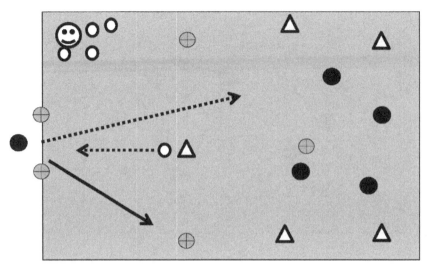

Set-Up: Cone off a small kickball field with four bases. Use two cones about 5 feet apart for the "home plate".

Game: Do NOT divide the players into two teams – just have one "kicker" and insure that each and every player gets his/her turn to participate in the game. Play basic kickball by the rules using hands. Any player that scores or is on base when a run is scored gets a point.

Coaching Points: Just play for 8 or 10 minutes to "set the tone for practice." Might even start right before the practice officially starts and add kids as they walk up.

Try to have fun with the players – spread them out if they are not familiar with the basic game of kickball and they all will want to be the pitcher!

Adjustments: Tell them if they do not catch the ball in the air for an "out" they must retrieve it only with their feet, and get the ball back in before it may be picked up with hands to tag a player out or throw to a base. Have fun!

In the second part of Warm-up, you may introduce an actual soccer ball but you do not have to do so, especially in the early phases of a season. You may wish to simply continue the first phase activity for the entire Warm-up without a ball. That is not a problem, especially if the players are having a good time! Below, see an example of an activity where a ball is used.

Diagram 3 – Toe Touches / Foundations (Warm-up)

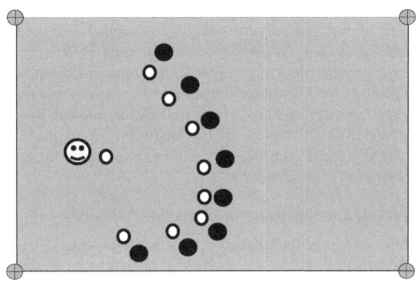

Set Up: Find an open area of your practice field and make sure each player has a ball along with you the coach – to demonstrate. Have the players with their ball facing you in a line or semi-circle.

Game: This warm-up activity could be performed at every practice. "Toe Touches" are where the player leaves the ball in front of her on the ground and lightly touches the top of it with the bottom of her toe in alternate foot fashion. The ball should barely move if at all. The coach starts the players by command and allows the player to touch the ball as many times as possible in a 15 to 20-second period. "Foundations" are where the player places the ball between his feet and, upon the coach's command, simply moves the ball back and forth from right foot to left foot using the inside of the foot – really the side/arch of the foot, as the contact point. Again, this is for 15 to 20-second time periods and the players should count repetitions and compete for the highest number.

Coaching Points: These activities teach soft touch and control of the ball at an early age which is an essential skill for all players. Do two sets of each then move on to your next activity. With the foundations, make sure the players bend their knees and do not try this activity with straight legs.

Adjustments: Longer time periods of up to 30 seconds as the players get older and stronger.

These two activities together (or just one if you want) generally should last no more than 10 to 12 minutes of the time allotted for the session. However, for your first practice or two you might spend up to 15 minutes in this area just to build the confidence of the kids in an activity that they are more familiar with and one they can play pretty well without having to learn anything new. Also, you can use this Warm-up part of practice to evaluate the athleticism of your players - how they run, jump, and their level of coordination.

Small-Sided Activity and/or Individual Ball Skills

After a short water break, your next activity is the main focus of your practice session - a small-sided game and/or individual ball skill. Again, in Chapters 5 and 6 you are provided with many of these activities.

"Small-sided" activities at this age typically involve a 1 v. 1 or 2 v. 2 player situation - and usually not the 4 v. 4 that the players may experience in more of a scrimmage format for kids of this age. If you are focusing more on an *individual ball skill* (such as a dribbling technique where you are encouraging players not to use their toes to push the ball) you can conduct these activities in a full group because the kids are really working hard on the skill without paying much attention to what is happening around them.

Why play "small-sided" games at this age, don't the older kids play 8 v. 8 and the adults play 11 v. 11? Good question. The simple answer is: Small-sided games and practice activities allow all players to come into contact with the ball more frequently than they would if they played in two larger groups. In a game of 11 v. 11 or even 8 v. 8 at this age, the number of touches and the duration of ball possession go down 50 to 70 percent on average compared to the recommended 3 v. 3 and 4 v. 4 formats.

Less contact with the ball means that the player's ball skills will develop slower than that of the kid who has ball contact two or three times more frequently. More touches = more skill with the ball. At the U6/U8 levels it is recommended that "games" consist of 3 v. 3 or 4 v. 4 players, small goals and no goalkeepers . . . and now you know why!

In this second phase of the practice session, you will be working primarily on the basic ball skills such as dribbling, kicking/shooting, controlling the ball with the inside of the foot and, possibly, some very short passing if you feel that a few of your players are ready for it. Do not rush things in your anxiety to prove that you are a good coach!

Your U8 players should be ready to learn how to pass the ball, or at least how to make short passes; and should acquire more advanced ball control skills. Try to measure your players' development and teach them accordingly. Review the player characteristics in Chapter 2 to determine the levels of your players.

Here are a few examples of appropriate practice activities for the Small-Sided and Individual Ball Skills portion of your practice sessions:

Diagram 4 – Line Soccer

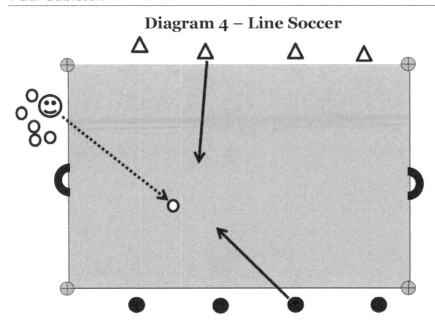

Set Up: Cone off a 15 x 20 yard grid and place small goals at each end. Divide the players into two teams and use colored pinnies to separate the teams. The team members should be assigned an individual number 1 – 4 or 5 (depending on your numbers) by the coach. Thus, two teams of four should be numbered 1 through 4 each. Line the players up for each team on opposite side lines so that #1 is facing #4 on the opposite team, #2 is facing #3, etc. Coach should have all the balls at his feet. Assign a goal for each team to attack.

Game: The coach calls out a number, such as #2 and serves a ball with a push pass into the middle of the field (see above). The two players assigned #2 should enter the field immediately upon hearing their number called, fight to win the ball, and try to dribble to their assigned goal to take a shot. The player that does not win the ball must defend his goal and try to win the ball or at least prevent a goal from being scored. If the ball goes out of bounds or past the goal, that session is over, players return to their starting points and a new number is called out.

Coaching Points: Encourage quick movements to the ball to win it or to close down defensively. Let the players be creative in dribbling to score a goal – they will figure out what works and what does not work. (If numbers are uneven, or to change the match ups, simply call out a specific number for each team – like "red 4 and yellow 5"). Try to match up evenly skilled players.

Adjustments: Eventually, call out two numbers and allow 2 v. 2 sessions to occur and even three numbers for 3 v. 3.

Diagram 5 – Small Sided, 2 v. 2, 3 v. 3, etc.

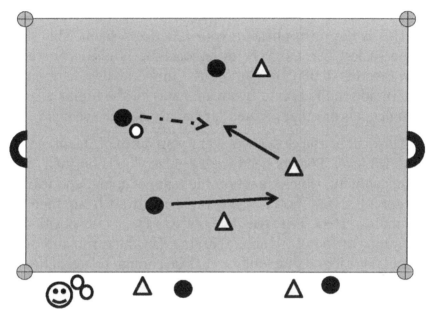

Set Up: Cone off a grid of approximately 15 x 20 yards with a small goal at each end. Divide your players into two teams with separately colored pinnies.

Game: This is basically a small-sided scrimmage where you can play 2 v. 2 or 3 v. 3 or 4 v. 4 depending on the numbers you have on your team or at practice that day. Simply let them play to score a goal as assigned. The coach should have a supply of balls and roll them in as needed. You can rotate in new players every minute or two to keep them fresh but without too much sideline sitting.

Coaching Points: Try to focus on only one or two points that you covered earlier in your practice session such as close dribbling, ball control or defensive positioning and see how the players are using a new skill or if they have learned it properly. Do not over coach here – let them play!

Adjustments: You may have a neutral player that is always offense and trying to score. Indicate that player with a third colored pinnie. So you play 2 v. 2 (red v. blue) with a third player (yellow) that is always on offense. Require that at least two players must touch the ball before the team can score – but do not over coach this as simply dribbling straight to goal is a great asset at this age!

"Free Play" Or Team Play

This is the third phase of your practice session. This should be the easiest because very little coaching is needed here. You allow the kids to play the game with limited involvement on your part. Divide the kids into two teams and let them play a "game" to small goals or other defined "areas" as you will see below.

This will be the closest you get to any form of "team" concept at the U8 level. Players need to recognize who is on their "team" for this activity, which direction the team is going, and learn the concept of trying not to take the ball away from their own teammates. **Pro Tip 10:** Do not worry about positions or formations or too much about passing. Let them run and dribble the ball, kick it and, hopefully, get close enough to a goal to take a shot.

What is all the fuss about "free play?" What exactly is it? You have already heard the term a few times in this book and probably elsewhere if you have researched about coaching younger children. Here kids get to play with a soccer ball without interference by the coach or supervision of the other adults present. Sometimes it requires goals and other objects to be set up, but it is largely played all over the world without props. Kids play pick-up games at school recess; some play street soccer after school; and some before practice, and between games on weekends.

Free play is crucial to the development of young soccer players. The opportunity for young players to try new things with the ball at their feet should be maximized. Free play creates a love for the game and a flair for overcoming challenges faced in the game.

Practice under the supervision of a coach in the traditional sense will always be important. But a player at times needs to break away from coach-oriented practice to honor an urge from within to play and improve without having to seek expert help.

The desire to improve must come from within the players as they grow older although it germinates at a young age. Free play prepares the groundwork for it.

This last phase of practice should whet their appetite for more and prepare them to take part in the weekly "game" or event. **Pro Tip 11:** Do not over-coach in this phase. Simply fix some parameters for them such as "stay in bounds," "do not use your hands," "try to score in 'that goal'" (while you point to it) etc. Encourage them to have fun within those basic rules. This part of the practice session should last about 10 to 15 minutes.

Here are a few examples of practice activities, in addition to a basic scrimmage, for Free Play:

Diagram 6 – Free Play/Small Sided – End Zones

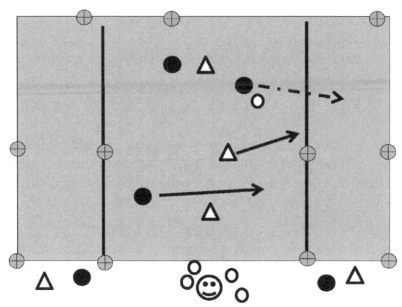

Set Up: Cone off a grid of approximately 20 x 30 yards with an "end zone" of approximately 4 yards deep at each end. Divide your players into two teams with separately colored pinnies.

Game: This is basically a small-sided scrimmage where you can play 2 v. 2 or 3 v. 3 or 4 v. 4 depending on the numbers you have on your team or at practice that day. Simply let them play to score a "touchdown" in the assigned end zone by dribbling or passing into the end zone with the ball under control. The coach should have a supply of balls and roll them in as needed. You can rotate in new players every minute or two to keep them fresh but without too much sideline sitting. You can start by requiring players to dribble into the end zone and stop the ball under control for a touchdown.

Coaching Points: Ball must be possessed and under control in the end zone to score. This works as a "free play" activity with the larger number of players involved. Try to focus on only one or two points that you covered earlier in your practice session such as close dribbling, ball control, or defensive positioning and see how the players are using a new skill or if they have learned it properly. Do not over coach here – let them play!

Adjustments: After dribbling into the end zone for points you can add that a player may pass to a teammate in the end zone where his teammate must control the ball in the end zone for a point. Again, add a neutral player that is always offense and trying to score. Indicate that player with a third colored pinnie. So you play 2 v. 2 (red v. blue) with a third player (yellow) that is always on offense. Require that at least two players must touch the ball before the team can score – but do not over coach this as simply dribbling/passing straight to goal is a great asset at this age.

Diagram 7 – Keep Away

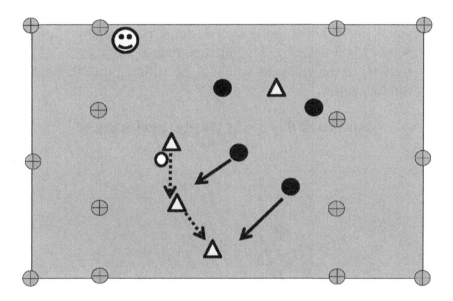

Set Up: Cone off a grid of approximately 15 x 25 yards. Add end zones of 5 yards deep at each end. Divide the players into two teams marked by colored pinnies. One ball.

Game: This simple warm-up game is a great way to start a practice. Allow the players to pick up the ball with their hands. Each team plays keep away from the other team within the grid and by tossing the ball to their teammates. Once a player catches the ball she may take no more than three steps before she must toss it to another teammate. The object of the game is to get the ball into your end zone for a point. You can allow 1 point for a successful pass to a teammate and 3 points for an actual score in the proper end zone. If the ball hits the ground more than once or goes out of bounds, the other team takes over. Defensive players can only intercept the ball when tossed and cannot take it out of a player's hands once caught.

Coaching Points: The focus here is to introduce to the players the idea of moving for passes and marking, or guarding, an opponent in order to win the ball. It also is a simple game to encourage the players to run, have fun without the pressure of soccer skills, and to develop athletically.

Adjustments: If you have small goals you can set them up at each end and require the teams to throw the ball into a goal for the 3 points instead of entering the end zone. You can also allow the 3 points when entering the end zone only upon a successful pass received in the end zone – that is, no running into the end zone with the ball.

Diagram 8 – 4 v. 4 Game/Scrimmage

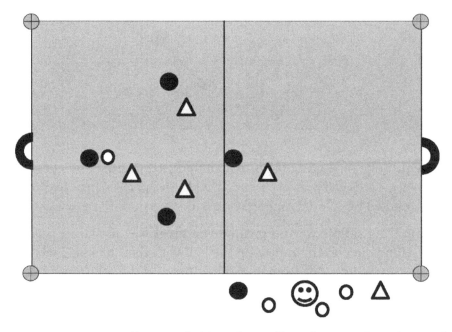

Set Up: Use a small game field with small goals at each end. Divide the players into two teams of four or five each. Put them in different colored pinnies.

Game: Let them play a "game" and try to score goals. Either play all your players or substitute as needed if players get too tired. Use a "neutral" player who is always offense if numbers are uneven.

Coaching Points: Really, just let them play. Encourage all players to get involved and do not worry about "left" and "right" side assignments – just let them find the ball and respond accordingly when possession changes from your team to the other team.

Wrap Up - End of Practice

At the end of each practice session the coach should summarize what the players have learned that day. Do not make a long speech — they will not have patience for it. Or you can recap by asking them a few questions for a minute or two: "What did we work on today?" (answer - dribbling), "Which parts of the foot can we use to dribble?" (answer - inside, outside and laces), etc. **Pro Tip 12:** Try to be positive and indicate what they should DO and not so much on what they should not do.

Have the players huddle together and let them stretch their hands out to touch the others' hands. After a count up to "three" they should say their team name in a loud chorus (e.g., "Tigers"). You may suggest using positive words such as "Play Hard" or "Pride." End the day on a positive note.

As promised, here are two practice sessions complete with a Warm-Up, Small-Sided/Individual Ball Skills Activity and Free Play Activity:

SAMPLE PRACTICE SESSIONS

Complete Practice Session 1:

<u>A Warm-Up:</u>

Diagram 9 – Leap Frog (Athleticism)

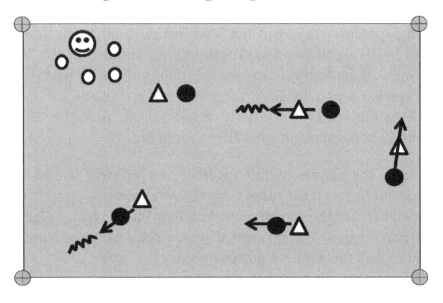

<u>Set Up:</u> Find an open area in your practice field. Have the players pick a partner so they are in groups of two. No balls needed at first.

<u>Game:</u> This activity is to develop general athleticism and confidence by the players. In pairs and on the coach's command, have the players play the classic leap frog game where one player squats down and the other player jumps over in a straddling manner. Players alternate this jumping activity so both players get plenty of repetitions. After a few rotations of classic leap frog start adding some additional movements. For instance, after the leap, have the leaping player perform a front roll before he then squats for his partner to do the same. Instead of a leap, have the first partner stand tall and spread his legs and the partner crawl through quickly and then jump straight up into the air, etc. If team numbers are uneven a group of three players works too.

Coaching Points: These activities simply prepare the players to play other more "soccer-like" games in a few moments but they should improve the players' athletic skills that will be needed as a soccer player. It also gives less experienced players some confidence in activities that do not involve a ball.

Adjustments: These are simple warm-up activities but eventually you can a add a ball to each pair and have them do the same type of leap frogging, front rolls, jumping, etc. but also have to generally keep up with a rolling soccer ball at their feet. They will love it!

B. Small-Sided Activity/Individual Ball Skills:

Diagram 10 – Chase

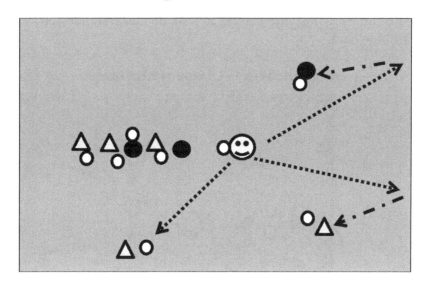

Set Up: Each player needs a ball and the coach uses an open area on the practice field. Cones and a precisely defined area are not needed. Players form a line facing coach.

Game: Each player has a ball and one by one hands ball to coach in the center of practice area. Coach simply tosses or kicks ball approximately 10 to 15 yards away into random areas. Players retrieve ball chasing it down, stopping it, and dribbling back to the coach or line. Don't worry the "line" will disappear almost immediately as the players start chasing their ball.

Coaching Points: Keep the players moving fast here. In the beginning and with very inexperienced players you could have the players chase the ball and pick it up with hands and return it to you as quickly as possible just to introduce the movement to the players. Then, introduce the stopping and dribbling skills. Focus on keeping the ball close as the player needs to control it more but allow for more distance between player and ball in the open field after the player first retrieves it.

Adjustments: You can throw/kick the ball farther for the more accomplished players and shorter for the less experienced players as needed. Later, you can set up gates and require the players to dribble through 1 or 2 gates before they return to you (See Diag. 1A below). Finally, the coach can move around after she throws the ball to require the players to look up and find her before they dribble back.

Diagram 10A – Chase with Gates

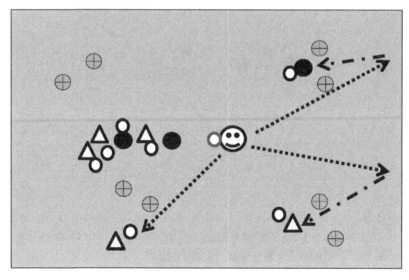

[End Diagram 10A]

C. Free Play or Team Play:

Diagram 11 (5 from above) – Small Sided, 2 v. 2, etc.

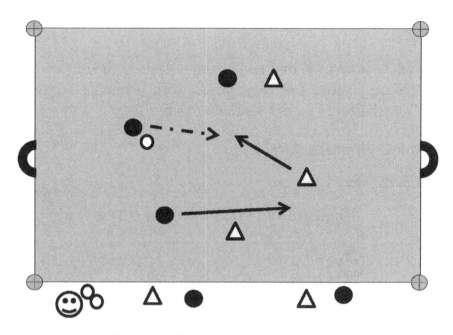

Set Up: Cone off a grid of approximately 15 x 20 yards with a small goal at each end. Divide your players into two teams with separately colored pinnies.

Game: This is basically a small-sided scrimmage where you can play 2 v. 2 or 3 v. 3 or 4 v. 4 depending on the numbers you have on your team or at practice that day. Simply let them play to score a goal as assigned. The coach should have a supply of balls and roll them in as needed. You can rotate in new players every minute or two to keep them fresh but without too much sideline sitting.

Coaching Points: Try to focus on only one or two points that you covered earlier in your practice session such as close dribbling, ball control or defensive positioning and see how the players are using a new skill or if they have learned it properly. Do not over coach here – let them play!

Adjustments: You may have a neutral player that is always offense and trying to score. Indicate that player with a third colored pinnie. So you play 2 v. 2 (red v. blue) with a third player (yellow) that is always on offense. Require that at least two players must touch the ball before the team can score – but do not over coach this as simply dribbling straight to goal is a great asset at this age!

D. Wrap-Up:

Talk to your team and review the lessons of the day and give them some positive feedback. Break with a huddle and a "go team" or whatever you like for them to say.

Complete Practice Session 2:

A. Warm-Up:

Diagram 12 (1 from above) – Tag

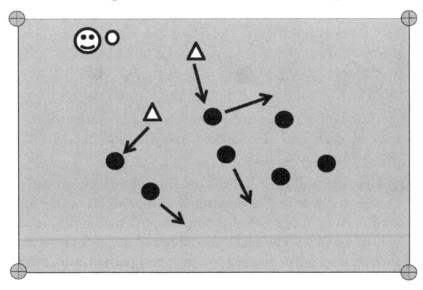

Set-Up: Find an open area approximately 20 x 30 yards in size. Cones are not necessary unless you think you need them. Place two players in the same colored pinnies

Game: This is a warm-up game and simply involves playing the classic game of tag and/or freeze tag if your kids like that one better. No ball is needed. The two players ("it") wearing pinnies seek out all other players and try to tag them. Once tagged a player becomes "it" and the old "it" player hands over the pinnie to the new one and runs away from her. If you play "freeze tag" you need the same set-up as above but once a player is tagged she must "freeze" in place and the two tagging players seek out the remaining players until all are tagged and frozen.

Coaching Points: This is simply a fun warm-up for the players to do and it does not require soccer skills at all. It develops basic athleticism of the players as they run, cut and dodge one another. Make the space smaller (with cones) if the tagging players are struggling.

Adjustments: This is a good practice starter to help set the tone for the remainder of a session. A other version of this classic game is that once a player is "tagged" she is added to the number of "taggers" and you keep tagging new players and adding them until the last player remains – who is the winner.

Diagram 13 – Simon Says

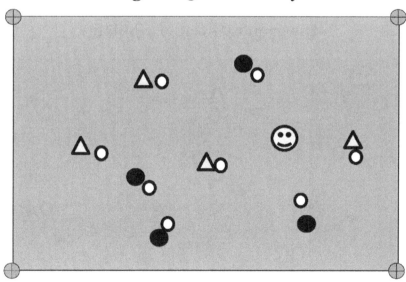

Set Up: You simply find an open area of approximately 15 x 20 yards. You may cone off or not at your choice. Each player needs a ball.

Game: Following the classic child's game of "Simon Says" the coach gives the players directions such as "Simon Says dribble". The players follow the directions. Then the coach instructs the players to stop the ball with a body part – like the foot, the elbow, even the head (for fun!). Also, instruct the kids to dribble only with their left foot, right foot, inside of feet, outside of feet, etc.

Don't forget the "game" portion of this exercise – if the coach doesn't say "Simon Says" and the players still do the task – then they have to do something funny like a front roll, or 5 jumps, or dribble around a distant cone, make an animal noise, etc. You decide.

Coaching Points: Instead of "Simon Says" you can make it "Coach (Your Name Here) Says" to better personalize the game. Work on skills that the players need to work on such as dribbling and ball control. This is a great warm-up activity.

Adjustments: Keep it simple and have fun! By altering the speed of the commands the players can be tested fairly keenly with this game.

B. Small-Sided Activity/Individual Ball Skills:

Diagram 14 – Gate Dribbling

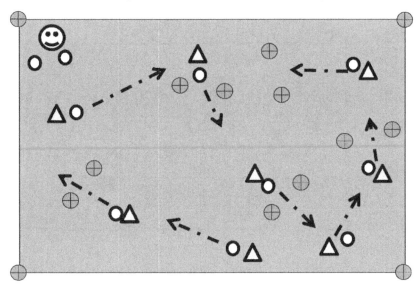

Set Up: Use a 15 x 20 yard grid. Add five or six cone gates (two cones about two yards apart) within the grid. Each player should have a ball.

Game: Upon the coach's command, players start dribbling inside the grid and try to dribble through as many gates as possible within the time period set by the coach of 1 to 3 minutes (based on age and ability). Players may not dribble through the same gate twice in a row.

Coaching Points: Encourage the players to look for an open gate and move from gate to gate as quickly as possible. Focus on the players keeping the ball close and under control. The ball may be farther from the feet when moving at speed between gates but closer to the feet when moving between the gates. Avoid allowing players to use their toes and encourage touches with the inside and outside of the feet and the laces. Teach players to keep their head up to see the activity around them.

Adjustments: Increase the time periods as the players become more confidant. Add restrictions such as only use the inside of feet, or outside of feet, left foot only. Encourage players to change speed and accelerate once through a gate until they reach the next gate, have them perform a simple "move" (e.g., step over) in between gates, etc. On your command, have them stop, then start again, do a turn, etc. as they navigate the gates.

C. Free Play or Team Play:

Diagram 15 (6 from above) –
Small Sided/Free Play – End Zones

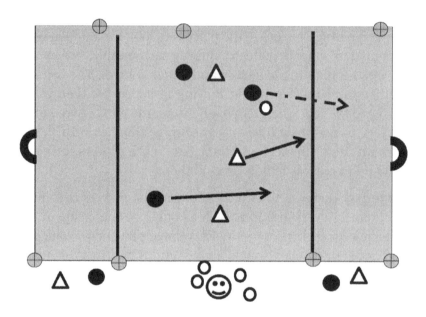

Set Up: Cone off a grid of approximately 20 x 30 yards with an "end zone" of approximately 4 yards deep at each end. Divide your players into two teams with separately colored pinnies.

Game: This is basically a small-sided scrimmage where you can play 2 v. 2 or 3 v. 3 or 4 v. 4 depending on the numbers you have on your team or at practice that day. Simply let them play to score a "touchdown" in the assigned end zone by dribbling or passing into the end zone with the ball under control. The coach should have a supply of balls and roll them in as needed. You can rotate in new players every minute or two to keep them fresh but without too much sideline sitting. You can start by requiring players to dribble into the end zone and stop the ball under control for a touchdown.

Coaching Points: Ball must be possessed and under control in the end zone to score. This works as a "free play" activity with the larger number of players involved. Try to focus on only one or two points that you covered earlier in your practice session such as close dribbling, ball control, or defensive positioning and see how the players are using a new skill or if they have learned it properly. Do not over coach here – let them play!

Adjustments: After dribbling into the end zone for points you can add that a player may pass to a teammate in the end zone where his teammate must control the ball in the end zone for a point. Again, add a neutral player that is always offense and trying to score. Indicate that player with a third colored pinnie. So you play 2 v. 2 (red v. blue) with a third player (yellow) that is always on offense. Require that at least two players must touch the ball before the team can score – but do not over coach this as simply dribbling/passing straight to goal is a great asset at this age.

D. Wrap-Up:

Again, talk to your team and review the lessons of the day and give them some positive feedback. Break with a huddle and a "go team" or whatever you like for them to say.

Chapter 5

HOW TO TEACH
TECHNIQUES AND SKILLS

There are basically four areas where you should concentrate your coaching efforts: general athleticism, dribbling, kicking/shooting, and defending. If you have more advanced players on your U6 team, or if you feel they are ready for more advanced techniques as the season moves forward, you can introduce passing and ball control. For the U8 group, these two skills should be introduced straightaway and practiced regularly along with the other basic skills.

At the end of each sub-section you will be given a few sample activities to show how to teach a specific skill. In Chapter 6 we will provide you with several activities for each specific skill discussed below. Do not worry, it is all here in the book for easy reference!

There are several "approaches" that a coach may use to teach techniques and skills to his players. Important among them are the demonstration approach, freeze method, and simply talking or explaining things to players. For the U6 and U8 players, the best approach by far is the demonstration method. This is where the coach or a model player demonstrates the technique, movement, or activity being taught.

In the freeze method, the coach tells the players to "freeze" during an activity. With the situation and, specifically, players' positions "frozen," it becomes easier for the coach to teach them what should have been the right move and what particular skill should have been applied under the circumstance. The scope of this technique, however, is limited in the case of U6 or U8 players — they are typically too young for it. It can be used with more success at older age levels.

As mentioned previously, the lecture method does not work very well for the U6 and U8 age groups. Players in these age groups are more inclined to watch a coach demonstrate a skill than listen to a verbal explanation of how it should be applied. They will simply get bored listening to you even if your lecture is precise and to the point. The coach should, however, interact verbally more with his U8 players, encouraging them to ask more questions.

BASIC TECHNIQUES

1. General Athleticism.

The importance of athleticism cannot be ignored. Coaches need to focus on the general coordination of their U6 and U8 players. The focus also should include running, jumping, testing balance/agility, twisting and moving. These activities should be of fairly short duration and may, at times, include a ball.

The improvement of the players' general athleticism is something that the coach should work on as it will later enhance the development of more specific skills. Coordination and athleticism are key components of advanced soccer skills.

Key Coaching Points - General Athleticism:

As you review and teach the skills and techniques to your players in order to improve their general athleticism, please keep these fundamentals in mind and *keep them simple*:

Running:

- Players should stand fairly straight so that they have a clear view of the ball and the field.

- The overall posture should be upright but when running fast it is natural for a player to lean slightly forward.

- Make sure the knees are bent and the thighs are moving upward and high during a sprint.

- When sprinting, the player should run primarily on the balls of his feet.

- The arms should be bent at the elbows in the shape of an L and the forearms should be moving back and forth in the direction that the player is running.

Jumping:

- Players should always keep the knees and ankles of their feet aligned.

- They should not allow the knees to buckle inward or outward or go out of line with the foot and ankle. This practice helps the players avoid knee injuries later in their careers.

- They must try to have a noticeable knee bend when pushing off and it helps them absorb the impact of landing following a jump.

- If pushing off on one foot, they should make sure the knee of the other is bent and pulled up high in order to propel themselves.

Previously referenced **Diagrams 1 (Tag), 7 (Keep Away), and 9 (Leap Frog)** are good activities to improve your players' athleticism.

2. Dribbling.

Learning how to dribble a ball may be the most important task for beginners. Without some knowledge of dribbling it is impossible to play soccer. **Pro Tip 13:** The best way to teach kids how to dribble is to allow them to have as much ball contact as possible during each and every training session.

Although you should allow players to develop their own styles of dribbling, you must teach them how to do it properly. The most fundamental aspects that should be taught are the points of contact with the foot and the distance the ball is allowed to travel from a contact point/player. Basically, dribbling requires the inside, outside and the top of a foot (or the laces of the shoe).

Many of the activities that you will see below and in Chapter 6 involve dribbling skills. On occasions, the coach may limit the number of contact points to be used during dribbling, For instance, ball contact may be allowed for some time using only the inside of the foot; and then, alternatively, only the outside of the foot.

Contacting the ball with the toe should not be encouraged. Although players do it instinctively it takes quite some doing to kick this bad habit. Why is the toe as a contact point a problem? Because it is difficult to dribble a ball efficiently by simply poking it with your toe. **Pro Tip 14:** "Say no to the toe" is a great chant to remind your players not to use theirs to dribble the ball.

At these age levels, a coach should introduce two basic styles of dribbling. One that is for tight or crowded spaces where the ball remains fairly close to the player's feet. The other is for full speed dribbling in open spaces where the ball is allowed to be farther away from the player's feet. The coach should try to help the player distinguish between the two types of dribbling.

Key Coaching Points - Dribbling:

• Tell players to focus on using the inside, outside, and the laces part of the foot to make contact with the ball.

• Encourage the players to dribble with both feet during activities and games.

• When dribbling, players should stay primarily on the balls of

63

their feet.

- While players at an early age must look down at the ball they are dribbling, try to encourage activities where they must keep their heads up, even if it is for a brief period, to look around to know where he/she wants to dribble and eventually pass or shoot the ball.

- The players should keep the ball close to their feet (1 yard or less) when dribbling in tight spaces and push the ball farther away (1 to 3 yards) when running at full speed and in open areas.

- Dribbling must be a primary activity in your training sessions at this stage.

Sample activities for dribbling:

Diagram 16 – Red Light / Green Light

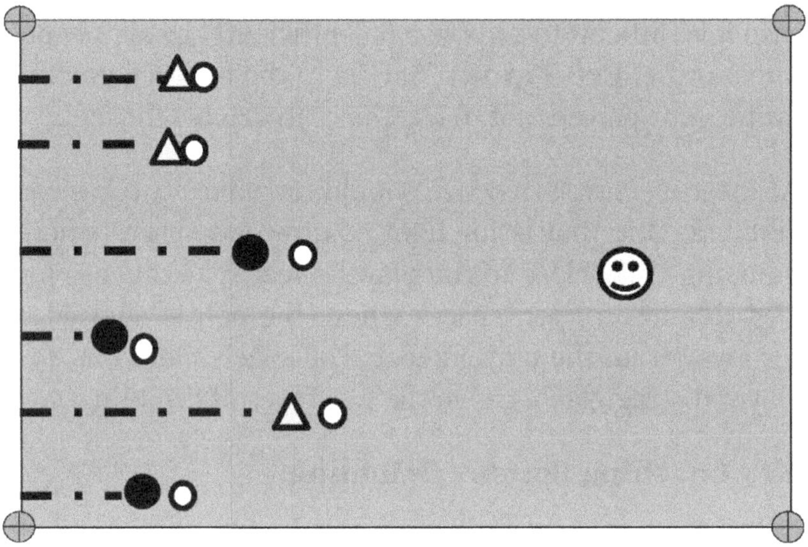

Set Up: Place corner cones in a 15 x 30 yard grid. Each player has a ball at his feet.

Game: This classic activity has been around forever. Line the players up on one endline with a ball and facing the coach. The coach yells "green light" and the players dribble straight ahead. The coach yells "red light" and the players stop immediately. The object for the players is to be the first to reach the other endline. If a player does not stop immediately when the coach yells "red light" then the coach should require such player to take three steps backwards.

Coaching Points: Focus on close control of the ball and using the inside of the foot and laces. As players develop add the outside of the feet as a contact point for the dribble. Also encourage the players to use both the left and right foot to dribble not just their favorite foot.

Adjustments: As players improve require them the look up when dribbling and not simply stare at the ball at their feet. Require the players to go all the way to the opposite endline, do a turn, and return using the green/red light commands. Require the players to only use their opposite foot to dribble for one length of the field, or use only the inside of their foot, or only the outside of their foot, etc.

Diagram 17 – Crossroads

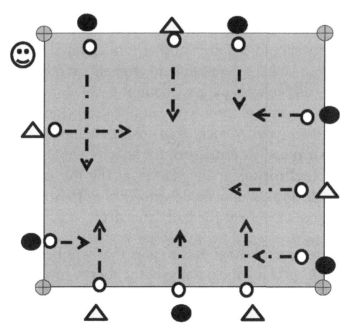

Set Up: Use a square area with corner cones approximately 12 x 12 yards. Place players on each side of the square with a ball at their feet. On your command, have the players dribble to the opposite side, turn around and dribble back to their starting point while avoiding other players.

Game: Each sideline the player touches counts as a point. Play for a minute and have the players count how many lengths they can cover before time runs out. (Each sideline counts as 1 so down and back would count as "2".)

Coaching Points: Focus on keeping the ball close with more touches when it gets busy in the middle areas and use fewer touches when more space is available. Quick turns will allow the players to earn more points.

Adjustments: Limit the players to inside of the foot only, outside of the foot only, left foot only, right foot only, etc. Direct the type of turn the player must perform – e.g., a pull back, an outside of the foot turn, a chop turn, etc. Try a larger square to give the players more room to operate in if they are struggling or if you want them to dribble for longer distances.

3. Kicking/Shooting.

Beginners should acquire another fundamental skill and that is the ability to kick a soccer ball and to shoot on goal. Obviously, it would be difficult to play without the ability to kick a ball accurately. For your players, you should keep things simple by focusing on two types of kicking: 1) using the inside of the foot, or the **"push pass" technique,** for shorter shots and 2) using the **instep technique** or the "laces" at the top of the shoe to strike the ball. Type 2 may be described as a traditional full kick toward the goal or to clear the ball defensively.

There are several other techniques that will be taught at an older age such as using the outside of the foot to propel the ball, a curving pass, a heel pass, a toe poke, etc. U6 and U8 players need to concentrate on the basic techniques that have been described in the previous paragraph before they learn the more advanced ways to move a ball.

We need to distinguish between the "push pass" technique as a method of kicking a ball and the concept of passing in general. Later in this chapter we will discuss the concept and execution of passing a ball from one teammate to another. The idea of passing the ball to a teammate is a fundamental one and some of your U6 players may be ready for it. All U8 players, however, should be introduced to short passing.

In this section the "push pass" technique is used as a manner of kicking the ball on goal or clearing it to safety - and not so much as a concept of distributing the ball to teammates. If your young players can learn the essentials of the technique, the next step of actually passing the ball to a teammate will be much easier for you to teach and for them to learn. As the players grow in skill, they will use both methods — push pass and instep kick — to pass to teammates, to shoot on goal, or to clear the ball defensively depending on the circumstances.

Kicking goes through three stages: The **preparation** (stepping up to the ball), **contact** between the foot and the ball, and the **follow through**. Your teaching and analyses of players' kicking techniques should revolve around these stages. Just remember though that young kids prefer a demonstration of a technique that they can copy, to an informative lecture on it. You can either kick the ball yourself for the demo or have an older and more experienced player do it for you.

Push Pass/Inside of Foot. Watch any high level soccer match for a few minutes and you will see repeated examples of the push pass technique of kicking. At the higher levels of soccer it is used to pass the ball between players over short and medium distances and to place a shot on goal when power is not needed. At the U6 and U8 levels, however, the push pass technique (or inside of the foot) should be used to propel the ball anywhere from two yards to as many as 8 or 10 yards. The ball should roll like a bowling ball and not jump into the air.

A young player should approach the ball from one or two steps directly behind it. The basic technique requires the player to place his/her non-kicking foot beside the ball about six inches away, with the toes of the planted foot pointing to the direction of the intended target. The kicking foot, fairly rigid in a 90° angle, takes the shape of an "L" with the toes pointing outward from the intended line of flight of the ball.

The point of contact with the ball is on the inside of the foot near the arch. Now most shoes have some stripes or logo close to this part; so it is easy for your players to locate and use that point on their shoes to make contact with the ball for a successful push pass. Ask them to keep their eyes on the ball while kicking it. They should strike the ball in its mid-section (not too far under it!) to keep it on the ground. Follow through to about shin high with the *knee of the kicking leg* bent and the thigh parallel to the ground. **Pro Tip 15:** *Do not allow* players to stab at the ball and leave their kicking foot on the ground instead of following through.

Instep Kick. The instep kick or drive is the standard full kicking motion that is used to take a shot on goal or to clear a ball a long distance away. For beginners, the contact point for an instep kick is the laces of the shoe as the foot strikes the middle of the ball. As players get older that contact point moves slightly to the inside part of the shoe laces. Instep kicks, even at these younger ages, can bring a ball a couple of feet off the ground and send it 10 to 20 yards away.

For a proper instep kick the player should start two or three steps behind the ball and slightly to the inside of it (i.e., not directly behind it). The kicker should stride up to the ball and place her non-kicking foot beside it at a distance of approximately 6-8 inches with the toes of the foot pointing in the direction of the target. The non-kicking leg should be slightly bent once it is planted next to the ball.

The knee of the kicking leg should be bent fairly sharply with the heel of the foot almost touching the buttocks. The toes should be pointing to the ground and locked in that motion during the kicking action. The kicking foot should strike the middle of the ball — the point of contact being that zone near the top of the laces of the shoe where the instep is rounded.

The follow through should be full with the kicking foot reaching knee level or higher. The toes of the kicking foot should be pointing straight down (like a ballerina) throughout the kick and briefly at the target at the peak of the follow through. Later, the players will be taught to land on their kicking foot after the ball is kicked. A full follow through in that manner, however, is not expected of most U8 players. They should be told simply to point the toes of their kicking foot to the target during this technique.

Key Coaching Points - Kicking/Shooting:

- Do not teach young kids by talking about how to kick a ball - demonstrate it!

- Analyze the players' preparation, contact points, and follow through techniques but teach by demonstration.

- Avoid lines as much as possible during your activities so that the players get more repetitions.

- Allow the players to break up into pairs and kick the ball to one another while you observe and correct them.

- Don't forget the hands and the arms — they should be extended and used for balance.

- Start with a still ball to teach the basics but make sure your players have opportunities to kick a moving ball as well as one from the dribble.

Sample activities for kicking/shooting:

Diagram 18 – Sharpshooter

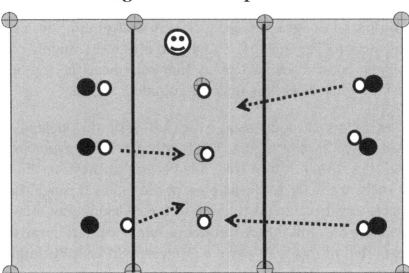

Set Up: Use a 20 x 15 yard grid. Create two end zone areas approximately 10 yards deep on each end as shown above. Place 3 to 5 flat cones in the middle of the grid with a ball balanced in the center of each cone. If more than six players then add a few more balls/cones. Divide the players into two teams and place one team in each end zone area. Each team should have three or four balls.

Game: Players try to knock a ball off of the cones in the center of the grid. The team that knocks off the most balls wins that round. The balls that miss a target in the middle should be controlled, set up, and a new shot taken by the opposing team.

Coaching Points: Focus on the accuracy of the player's kick or pass to the targeted balls on the cones. Also, encourage good control and set up of the ball by the players receiving a missed shot. You should adjust the distances according to skill and strength levels.

Adjustments: You may require the players to use the push pass technique (easier) or a full shot with the laces (harder). Require the players alternate the kicking foot once they get a feel for the game. Add a requirement that upon receipt of a ball, the player must dribble back to his endline (behind him), perform a turn and then dribble back to the edge of his end zone before he makes a pass/shot.

Diagram 19 – Whack – A – Coach

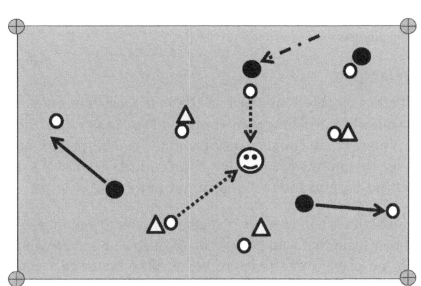

Set Up: All you need is an open area approximately 20 x 15 yards or so in size – cones are not necessary unless you want to use them to keep your players better contained. Each player needs a ball.

Game: Ask the players to start dribbling in the open area. On your signal when you say "go" or blow your whistle, the players try to hit you with their ball below your knees by kicking or "push passing" a ball at you. If they miss, the player must retrieve his own ball and try again. The coach should move around some to challenge the players. Award a point for each time a player successfully hits you with a ball below your knees. Play for 2 to 3 minutes per game and play several games.

Coaching Points: This activity has it all – dribbling, shooting, turning with the ball, and even passing if the player uses the push pass to hit you. Give positive feedback and simple instructions – like keep the ball low, keep the ball close before you shoot, etc.

Adjustments: You can add restrictions such as the shot must be taken from 3 steps away or further, only push passes for shots, only balls hit with the laces count for points – or maybe 2 points for a successful shot with the laces and 1 point for a successful push pass. Add a single defender to protect you by preventing shots if it becomes too easy to score. Become more of a moving target when you feel your players are ready for a greater challenge.

4. Defending.

Defensive play is the last of the four most important skills that you will be teaching your young players. In fact, "defending" seems more of a tactic than a skill and in some respects it is. The idea is to introduce some basic individual defensive skills - mostly positioning - to these beginning players.

Sometimes half or more of a game is spent defending against the other team that is in possession of the ball. So the sooner you teach the players the basics of defense the better they play on both sides of the ball - offense and defense.

As the players grow up, they will be taught fundamental defensive skills such as turning sideways to defend a player 1 v. 1, avoiding stabbing or swiping at the ball, covering for a defending teammate, and the other aspects of defense. **Pro Tip 16:** At this stage of learning the defensive side of soccer, simply focus on the fundamentals of moving to the ball, positioning on the field when tracking an opposing player, and positioning the body sideways once reaching the ball. We will keep these basics extremely simple and so should you.

Moving to the Ball. At the professional level this is called "pressuring" the player in possession of the ball. It is difficult for a team to defend itself if at least one of its players is not close to the opponent(s) holding the ball. At the beginner stage, the basic idea to convey is that if the defending team does not have the ball then one or more of its players need to go and get it back. It is that simple - "go get the ball."

Encourage each player to try to win the ball back but not to "get in the way of" his/her own teammates also trying to do so. Once a player goes for the ball he needs to be under control as he comes to face the player in possession of it. Only through a well-controlled approach can he accurately take the ball away from the opposing player or clear it with a hard kick. **Pro Tip 17:** A popular chant for older players on this defensive approach is "fast, slow, low and go." Meaning, move "fast" to the ball, "slow" down as you take the last step or two to reach the player possessing it, get "low" as you approach the ball, and then "go" for the ball.

Do not "over-coach" and deter players from moving to the ball just because someone else on their own team might be closer. If one player gets to the ball first he has obviously performed well. You can use this as an example to motivate others to be fast enough to win the ball. Soccer wisdom says the player nearest to the opponent holding the ball should move first to get it, but that requires some experience and thinking which will develop later. Right now just let the kids attack the ball.

Tracking the Ball. The players must be encouraged to attack the ball when their opponents are in possession of it. Later in their development they will learn how to deal with the situation patiently and not to stab or recklessly swipe at the ball. For now, you must focus on the development of your players demonstrating how to run at the opposing player holding the ball and how to chase and catch a player who has moved past the defender. It is fairly straight forward.

We talked about "moving to the ball" when it is in front of the defender. The player moves quickly to the ball, slows somewhat as he gets to it, and then tries to win it. Things, however, change when the dribbler is near the sideline and the defender is farther away from the ball. As adults, we can realize that the defender cannot move where the dribbling player is, but he/she must shift to the place the dribbler is headed. This is not always an easy thing to do for young players.

How track a dribbler from several yards away? You must show the defender through demonstration how quickly to move to the spot the dribbling player wants to reach. The defender must arrive at the spot first to face the oncoming dribbler. Now he can focus on winning the ball. This is a concept that you can best show by demonstration and with the help of some activities given below - some with a ball, some without.

Diagram 20 – Defensive Angles

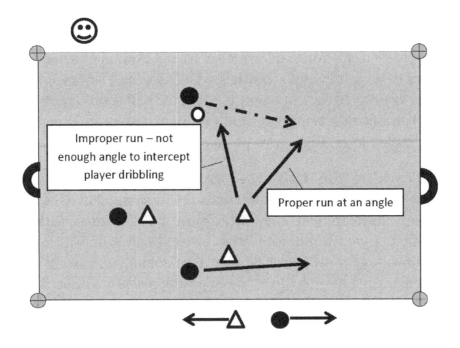

As for the key defensive concept of "patience," you will have to show some of yours in not over-emphasizing it at the U6 and U8 levels. Certainly, you do not want to weaken the spirit of some players that have the raw talent to move faster than others and outright win a loose ball. Not all players will be equally gifted with speed but the ones that are fast, need to learn from a very young age how to use that talent effectively – learning to be patient can come later.

Sideways Body Position. Not a big deal at these ages, but if you have an opportunity to demonstrate to a defender moving sideways to an opposing player possessing the ball - as opposed to moving flat - then make good use of it. The idea at the higher levels of the game is that by moving sideways to defend a player in possession of the ball - that is, with a shoulder and a leg closer to the dribbling player than the chest - the defender can react better to the moves of the dribbler and can also force that player to a less dangerous position among other things. Few things are worse at the higher levels than a defender moving into a dribbling player completely "flat" and the dribbler simply outflanking him because his body position is all wrong.

When you feel the player or players are ready to learn this technique, simply show them that moving to the dribbling player quickly and then turning slightly sideways just before the dribbler is reached works better than arriving square or "flat." The defending player should look like a fencer or a surfer – moving back and forth with the body sideways. This imagery is helpful for young players.

Key Coaching Points - Defending:

- Focus on your players simply moving *to the ball* to defend and not waiting for the attacking player to come to them.

- When trying to win a ball in a 50/50 situation (i.e., either player could win it) encourage the defending player to form his/her attacking foot into the shape of an "L" (as in the side foot kick above) to move or sweep the ball away.

- Do not worry about or even try "man-to-man" marking or other higher level defensive tactics.

- You may spread your players out during your game activities insuring that at least one plays more defensively at times than the rest. But do not overdo it and rotate such player responsibilities.

- Use basic games (see Chapter 6) like "tag" and "shadow game" without a ball where players "defend" by chasing or mirroring another player - then add a ball and watch how the defenders excel!

Sample activities for defending:

Diagram 21 – Banana Run - Defense 1 v. 1

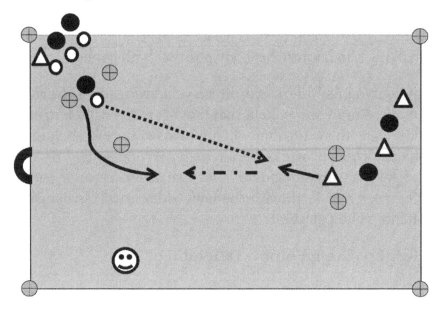

Set Up: Use a grid of approximately 20 x 25 yards with a small goal at one end. Place two cones (offensive) in the center about 20 yards from the small goal, another two cones (defensive) about 5 yards inside the endline and 5 yards inside the sideline, and, finally, a third cone (angle cone) about 5 yards from the defensive cone at an angle and slightly closer to the offensive cone – see above diagram for details.

Game: Arrange the players (no pinnies needed) with half behind the offensive cones and half behind the defensive cones facing the center of the field. The defensive player starts with the ball and serves it with a firm push pass to the feet of the first offensive player in line. The offensive player receives the ball, controls it, and immediately attacks the goal and tries to score. The defending player must run around the angle cone (far side) before she can defend the attacking player. Players alternate lines after each turn.

Coaching Points: No long shots but encourage the players to receive, control, dribble and then shoot with a firm push pass to score. The attacking player must dribble past the defending player in order to score. The defending player's run around the angle cone is sometimes called an "angled run" or you might just call it a "banana run" for fun because of its curved nature. The idea here is to teach players how to better position themselves when running to "close down" an attacking dribbler – encourage the defender to move quickly toward the ball in this manner.

Adjustments: Change sides from where the defenders start their runs from time to time (make sure you adjust the angle cone when you do). This game is good for attackers too – have them try "moves" and make sure they control the ball first before they start to dribble. If you have more than 10 players you can set this game up in both directions (using two separate goals) to avoid lines and waiting.

Diagram 22 (former 4 above) – Line Soccer

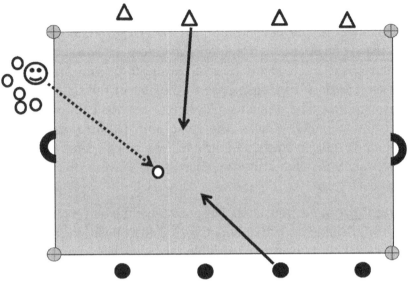

Set Up: Cone off a 15 x 20 yard grid and place small goals at each end. Divide the players into two teams and use colored pinnies to separate the teams. The team members should be assigned an individual number 1 – 4 or 5 (depending on your numbers) by the coach. Thus, two teams of four should be numbered 1 through 4 each. Line the players up for each team on opposite side lines so that #1 is facing #4 on the opposite team, #2 is facing #3, etc. Coach should have all the balls at his feet. Assign a goal for each team to attack.

Game: The coach calls out a number, such as #2 and serves a ball with a push pass into the middle of the field (see above). The two players assigned #2 should enter the field immediately upon hearing their number called, fight to win the ball, and try to dribble to their assigned goal to take a shot. The player that does not win the ball must defend his goal and try to win the ball or at least prevent a goal from being scored. If the ball goes out of bounds or past the goal, that session is over, players return to their starting points and a new number is called out.

Coaching Points: Encourage quick movements to the ball to win it or to close down defensively. Let the players be creative in dribbling to score a goal – they will figure out what works and what does not work. (If numbers are uneven, or to change the match ups, simply call out a specific number for each team – like "red 4 and yellow 5"). Try to match up evenly skilled players.

Adjustments: Eventually, call out two numbers and allow 2 v. 2 sessions to occur and even three numbers for 3 v. 3.

THE NEXT LEVEL - FOR SOME

The next two sub-sections introduce the basic techniques of ball control and passing. These skills are at a slightly higher level than the basic areas discussed above such as general athleticism, dribbling, kicking/shooting and defending. The basic areas should be taught to all players of the U6 and above groups. Although these two new elements require a higher level of athleticism and skill, I believe many players even at this early age are ready to learn them.

These two areas are appropriate for U8 and older players, and may be so for some more advanced learners on a U6 team which is not generally taught these techniques. So when some players on your team are ready for these skills and some are not, you need to arrange the ball control and passing activities in such way that the latter can still participate in these sessions in a positive manner.

5. Ball Control.

Ball control is merely the skill of receiving the ball on the ground, in the air, or from a bounce. Then controlling it in a manner that allows the player to dribble, pass or otherwise redirect the ball. Without the skill of ball control it is extremely difficult for teams in the older age groups to maintain possession of the ball both individually and collectively. Starting to learn the ins and outs of ball control at a young age will help players later in their careers.

The ball can come to a player in three ways: from the **ground**, a **bounce**, or the **air**. Although players can receive the ball on many different parts of their bodies, the basic points of contact are with the foot on the **inside** or **outside**, the **instep**, or the **sole**, and then the **"body"** (chest, thigh, head, etc.). The lists below enumerate the ball paths and contact points from "easier" to "harder":

Ball Paths		Contact Points
ground	Easier	inside of foot
		sole
bounce	to	instep
		outside of foot
air	Harder	'body' (chest, thigh, head, etc.)

This is a basic guideline as the "easier" to "harder" scale may be different for various players. For instance, one player may be very confident of controlling air balls on his chest rather than a bouncing ball with the outside of his foot. I think, however, this chart will be a great guide for a coach in teaching players how to control balls, coming in from various paths, with different contact points.

At the U6 age level and for those ready to learn the basics of ball control, you should start with using the inside of the foot to control ground balls. Next, move to the sole of the foot, then to the instep and, finally, the outside of the foot. The chart above is a good guide for the ground ball sequence too.

In sum, there are three ball paths (ground, bounce and air) and five contact points (inside, sole, instep, outside of foot, and the "body") for young players to learn. **Pro Tip 18:** Focus on two approaches for controlling the ball: the "trap" method (some like to call it a "wedge" or "roof") and the "soft touch" method (some call it a "cushion" or "elevator").

The **trap** method is a movement where the player essentially catches the ball between his foot and the ground - that is, he "traps" the ball between the two. In the **soft touch method** the player uses his foot or body to cushion the ball, or receive it softly by pulling back from it on contact — think of the ball hitting a pillow and remaining at your feet.

At the U6 age, I would not worry too much about air balls but you can try to work with some bouncing balls using the contact points in a slightly different order than given above. With bouncing balls, try this order — sole of foot ("trap"), instep and inside of foot ("soft touch"). The "elevator" is where a player cradles an air ball on his laces and brings it down to the ground under control.

The "body" control can come later, too, but you could show these young players some introductory basics about how to get in front of and in line with a bouncing ball with their chests and thighs. Simply have the players block a bouncing ball with their chests or thighs and allow it to fall to the ground.

Key Coaching Points - Ball Control:

- Use the above order of ball paths and contact points to introduce ball control.

- Using activities similar to the ones given below, refer to the "trap" method as "roofing" the ball. The players will understand this phrase quickly as it explains the concept with graphic precision. Show them how to put their foot on top of the ball (its "roof") to control it - always demonstrate it.

- When teaching players to trap a ball with the sole of their foot, have them point their toe up at a 45° angle (like a "wedge") and catch the ball under it. They should press on the ball slightly to insure that it stops cleanly; then they can pull the ball back a little toward them before taking the foot off the top of the ball to prepare for the next dribble or movement.

- When teaching players the soft touch method make sure you emphasize pulling back of the receiving foot to slow the ball down and control it. This can be performed on all surfaces making contact with the ball.

- When teaching players to control a bouncing or an air ball using the soft touch method, especially with the instep (top of the foot), refer to it as the "elevator" method. Show them how to cradle a ball in the air with their foot about knee high and then bring it down to the ground. The ball will touch the foot briefly on the way down. It is a good start on controlling air balls with a foot.

- Again, analyze the players' preparations, contact points, and follow through techniques for ball control but teach by demonstration.

Sample activities for ball control:

Diagram 23 – Circle Pass

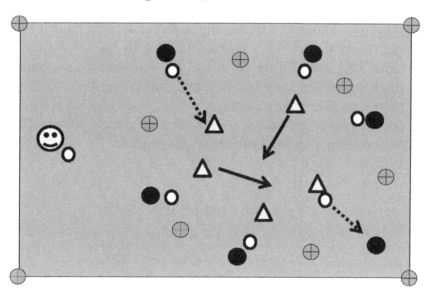

Set Up: Create a circular area using five or six cones with a diameter of approximately 15 yards. Divide your team into two even teams of four to six players. If you have more than 12 total players you may need to enlarge the circle by a few yards. Place one team on the outside in a circular shape in between the cones. Each outside

83

player should have a ball at his feet. Place the other players inside the circle without a ball.

Game: The players on the inside simply move toward an open outside player who serves the inside player a good push pass on the ground. The inside player receives the ball, controls it, and push passes it back to the same outside player. After passing back, the inside player then runs to another outside player to receive another pass and repeats. Inside players should move quickly from open outside player to player. Run for one to two minute time periods and then change the inside and outside players.

Coaching Points: This simple activity allows for many touches and repetitions on both push passes and controlling a moving ball. Focus the players on either a "soft touch" cushion control or a "trap" with the sole of the foot on top of the ball. On the push passes, concentrate on keeping the ball on the ground with the proper contact point using the middle of the inside of the foot on the middle of the ball.

Adjustments: You may require only push passes with the left foot or right foot. Control by a cushion only or by the sole of the foot only. After the players get a feel for this first phase, have the receiving player take the ball and turn it, dribble to another player, and then push pass it to a new, open outside player. The outside player will then serve it back to the inside player who will then receive it and move to yet another player.

Diagram 24 – Circle Ball Control – Air

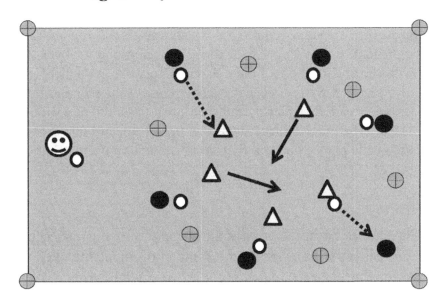

Set Up: Cone off a circular area using five or six cones with a diameter of approximately 15 yards. Divide your team into two even teams of four to six players. If you have more than 12 total players you may need to enlarge the circle by a few yards. Place one team on the outside in a circular shape in between the cones. Each outside player should have a ball in his hands. Place the other players inside the circle without a ball.

Game: The players on the inside simply move toward an open outside player who serves the inside player an underhanded tossed ball. The inside player receives the ball, controls it, and push passes it back to the same outside player. After passing back, the inside player then runs to another outside player to receive another tossed ball and repeats. Inside players should move quickly from open outside player to player. Run for one to two minute time periods then change inside and outside players.

Coaching Points: This simple activity allows for many touches and repetitions on both controlling an air ball and push passing it. Focus the players on either a "soft touch" cushion control or a "trap" with the sole of the foot on top of the ball. On the push passes, concentrate on keeping the ball on the ground with the proper contact point using the middle of the inside of the foot on the middle of the ball.

Adjustments: You may require only push passes with the left foot or right foot. Control by a "soft touch" cushion only or by a "trap" with the sole of the foot only. After the players get a feel for this first phase, have the receiving player control the ball and turn it, dribble to another player, and then push pass it to a new outside player. The outside player will then pick it up, and toss it back to the inside player who will then receive it and move to yet another player.

6. Passing.

The skill of passing includes all forms of moving a soccer ball from one player to another on the same team in a controlled way. The better the accuracy and control shown in delivering a ball the greater is the chance of the recipient to control the ball successfully. At the U6 stage, however, passing is not the most important skill but as the player grows older, it assumes importance for the team and the individual. In fact, it is a fundamental element of soccer that is developed throughout a player's career.

As with the skill of ball control, passing has many different techniques and options conditional to the following: 1) How does the player that will pass the ball **receive it** - from the air or on the ground? 2) Once the ball is received, what will be the passing player's **contact point** on his foot to deliver a pass - inside or outside of foot, instep, toe, heel? 3) Finally, how will the passing player choose to **deliver the ball** - in the air or on the ground?

While teaching passing techniques to U6 beginners, all a coach should focus on is short passing with the inside of the foot and the instep - such as with a shot on goal or a full kick. Most passes at the U6/U8 levels should be on the ground. Remember, passing is controlled delivery of the ball to another teammate - not simply kicking it away to anywhere. For these players the distance will typically be about 5 to 10 yards maximum. **Pro Tip 19:** *I recommend that you concentrate only on the **push pass** (inside of foot) and the **instep pass** ("laces").* Please review section 3 of this chapter, above, on Kicking and Shooting, including the Key Coaching Points, because these techniques are the same for passing at this age.

For U8 players, you should focus more on coordinated passing between players both at practices and during the games. Chapter 6 provides several good passing activities to help you introduce this skill to your players. Try to use activities that allow them to move freely with a ball and a partner or in groups of three while passing the ball among one another. These low-pressure passing activities also work as great warm-ups for young and older players.

In the Kicking and Shooting section, above, the fundamental elements of the **push pass** were introduced in sequence with the approach, contact, and follow through. In review, here are the basics to the push pass technique: **[Approach]** Non-kicking foot planted about six inches away from the ball with the toes pointed toward the intended target. **[Contact]** Kicking foot forms the shape of an "L" - fairly rigid in a 90° angle - and turned with the toes pointing outward. **[Follow through]** Lastly, the ball is kicked and the follow through made to about shin high with the kicking knee still bent and thigh parallel to the ground. *Do not allow* the player to stab at the ball and leave his kicking foot on the ground without following through.

The other age-appropriate passing technique is the **instep pass**. Again, review the section on Kicking/Shooting, above, for the basics. Here is a quick reminder of those fundamentals for the instep pass in the approach, contact, and follow through analysis: **[Approach]** The player should start at a slight angle behind the ball; then take two or three steps toward it; and place his/her non-kicking foot approximately 6 inches beside the ball, with a slightly bent knee and the plant foot toes pointing in the direction of the target. **[Contact]** The toes of the kicking foot should be pointed down (or straight like those of a ballerina) and locked in that motion during the kicking action and the kicking foot should make contact with the middle of the ball. **[Follow through]** The toes should remain pointed straight throughout a full kick and pointing at the target briefly at the peak of the follow through.

Key Coaching Points - Passing:

- As in teaching players how to pass a ball, keep talking to a minimum - demonstrate it (or if you can't do it, use other younger players - but older than your team – who have good techniques to help you out)!

- Analyze the players' approach, contact points, and follow through techniques but teach by demonstration.

- Allow the players to break up into pairs and kick the ball to one another while you observe and correct them as needed. By all means, avoid long and boring lines!

- Don't forget the hands and the arms - which should be extended and used for balance.

- Again, as with the shooting technique, start with a still ball to teach the basics but make sure your players have opportunities to pass moving balls especially from a dribble.

Sample activities for passing:

Diagram 25 – Gate Passing

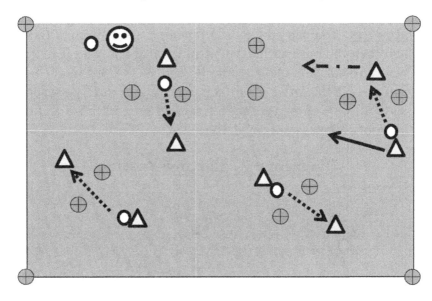

Set Up: Create a 15 x 20 yard grid. Add five or six cone gates (two cones about two yards apart) within the grid. Divide the players into pairs with 1 ball per pair.

Game: Have the players dribble the ball and pass back and forth with their partner. Upon your command have the players continue passing with their partner but now require the players to try to pass between as many different gates as possible within a 1 to 3 minute time span (based on age and ability). Players should keep count of the number of gates they pass between. Players may pass or dribble outside the gates to get into position but only the passes between the gates count toward their "score". Players may not pass between the same gate twice in a row. Team with the most passes through the gates is the winner.

Coaching Points: Encourage the players to move from gate to gate upon completion of a successful pass. Focus on the players keeping the ball on the ground and using good "push pass" technique. Make sure the kicking foot is in the shape of an "L" and non-kicking foot is pointed toward the target. Contact the middle of the ball and follow through. Also, make sure the players allow for enough space between their partner when passing – too close does not produce good passing results here or on the game field.

Adjustments: You can add an additional pass – 1 through the gates and then the receiver must control the ball and pass it right back before the players move to another gate – the "1-2 pass". Be sure you reverse the order of initial passing player after 30 seconds or so to allow both players to initiate and control the ball. Require left foot only passes through the gates.

Diagram 26 – Partner Passing

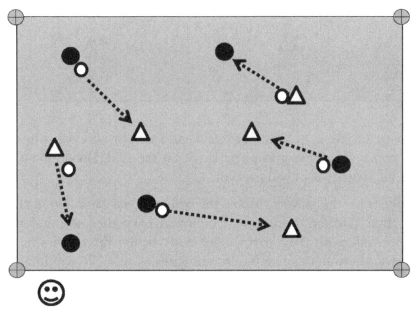

Set Up: Use an area of approximately 30 x 30 yards. Have the players find a partner with one ball between them.

Game: First, have the players push pass back and forth while standing about 6 yards apart to allow them to grasp the basic skills of push passing. Next, the players should move around the area and push pass the ball to their partner while moving. The partner should receive the ball and pass it back to the partner – all while moving around the designated area. Proceed for about two minutes and rest for a minute while you review the fundamentals of push passing with the players. This is a good warm-up activity too.

Coaching Points: Try to focus on the quality of the push pass. The pass should be on the ground and firm. Soft passes are not realistic for game conditions and do not work. Emphasize a good contact point with the inside of the foot and a good follow through.

Adjustments: Once comfortable with the basic skills of the push pass, add a combination pass where the receiving player first times the ball back to the first passer and then moves. The first passer then takes a few dribbles and delivers it again to the receiving player. After about 30 seconds, change the roles.

Chapter 6

MORE ACTIVITIES AND GAMES

U6 and U8 Activities - Athletic Games, Dribbling, Kicking / Shooting, Defending, Ball Control and Passing -Putting the Skills to Work

You will find below several useful soccer activities to use at your practices to teach your players the fundamentals of the game. These activities include the previously presented examples and additional activities for your use. They are arranged for your convenience by the skill or technique(s) that they promote. Many activities include more than a single skill set, such as dribbling *and* shooting, but are arranged with the most prominently required skill.

Remember, at the younger ages and especially in the U6 age group, the more of a "game" the activity is the greater the enjoyment for the players. Sometimes a creative "game element" or a story line is given below and, for other activities, you will need to come up with your own theme based on the needs of your team to make learning fun for your players.

The Diagrams are numbered according to their first appearance in the book if they occurred earlier. Here is a repeat of the key to the diagrams for your convenience:

Key to Diagrams

Activities for Athleticism:

Tag

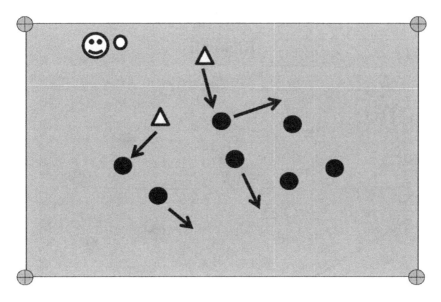

Set-Up: Find an open area approximately 20 x 30 yards in size. Cones are not necessary unless you think you need them. Place two players in the same colored pinnies

Game: This is a warm-up game and simply involves playing the classic game of tag and/or freeze tag if your kids like that one better. No ball is needed. The two players ("it") wearing pinnies seek out all other players and try to tag them. Once tagged a player becomes "it" and the old "it" player hands over the pinnie to the new one and runs away from her. If you play "freeze tag" you need the same set-up as above but once a player is tagged she must "freeze" in place and the two tagging players seek out the remaining players until all are tagged and frozen.

Coaching Points: This is simply a fun warm-up for the players to do and it does not require soccer skills at all. It develops basic athleticism of the players as they run, cut and dodge one another. Make the space smaller (with cones) if the tagging players are struggling.

Adjustments: This is a good practice starter to help set the tone for the remainder of a session. Another version of this classic game is that once a player is "tagged" she is added to the number of "taggers" and you keep tagging new players and adding them until the last player remains – who is the winner.

Kickball

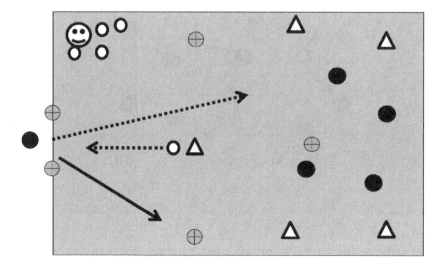

Set-Up: Cone off a small kickball field with four bases. Use two cones about 5 feet apart for the "home plate".

Game: Do NOT divide the players into two teams – just have one "kicker" and insure that each and every player gets his/her turn to participate in the game. Play basic kickball by the rules using hands. Any player that scores or is on base when a run is scored gets a point.

Coaching Points: Just play for 8 or 10 minutes to "set the tone for practice." Might even start right before the practice officially starts and add kids as they walk up.

Try to have fun with the players – spread them out if they are not familiar with the basic game of kickball and they all will want to be the pitcher!

Adjustments: Tell them if they do not catch the ball in the air for an "out" they must retrieve it only with their feet, and get the ball back in before it may be picked up with hands to tag a player out or throw to a base. Have fun!

Keep Away

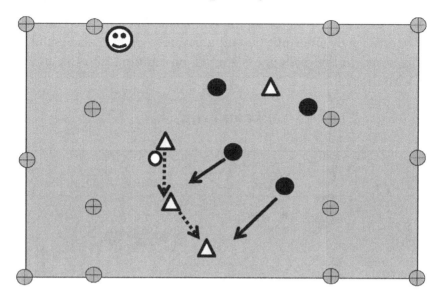

Set Up: Cone off a grid of approximately 15 x 25 yards. Add end zones of 5 yards deep at each end. Divide the players into two teams marked by colored pinnies. One ball.

Game: This simple warm-up game is a great way to start a practice. Allow the players to pick up the ball with their hands. Each team plays keep away from the other team within the grid and by tossing the ball to their teammates. Once a player catches the ball she may take no more than three steps before she must toss it to another teammate. The object of the game is to get the ball into your end zone for a point. You can allow 1 point for a successful pass to a teammate and 3 points for an actual score in the proper end zone. If the ball hits the ground more than once or goes out of bounds, the other team takes over. Defensive players can only intercept the ball when tossed and cannot take it out of a player's hands once caught.

Coaching Points: The focus here is to introduce to the players the idea of moving for passes and marking, or guarding, an opponent in order to win the ball. It also is a simple game to encourage the players to run, have fun without the pressure of soccer skills, and to develop athletically.

Adjustments: If you have small goals you can set them up at each end and require the teams to throw the ball into a goal for the 3 points instead of entering the end zone. You can also allow the 3 points when entering the end zone only upon a successful pass received in the end zone – that is, no running into the end zone with the ball.

Leap Frog

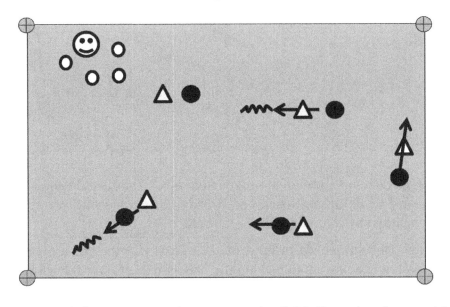

Set Up: Find an open area in your practice field. Have the players pick a partner so they are in groups of two. No balls needed at first.

Game: This activity is to develop general athleticism and confidence by the players. In pairs and on the coach's command, have the players play the classic leap frog game where one player squats down and the other player jumps over in a straddling manner. Players alternate this jumping activity so both players get plenty of repetitions. After a few rotations of classic leap frog start adding some additional movements. For instance, after the leap, have the leaping player perform a front roll before he then squats for his partner to do the same. Instead of a leap, have the first partner stand tall and spread his legs and the partner crawl through quickly and then jump straight up into the air, etc. If team numbers are uneven a group of three players works too.

Coaching Points: These activities simply prepare the players to play other more "soccer-like" games in a few moments but they should improve the players' athletic skills that will be needed as a soccer player. It also gives less experienced players some confidence in activities that do not involve a ball.

Adjustments: These are simple warm-up activities but eventually you can a add a ball to each pair and have them do the same type of leap frogging, front rolls, jumping, etc. but also have to generally keep up with a rolling soccer ball at their feet. They will love it!

Chase

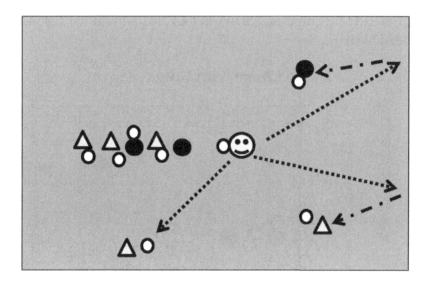

Set Up: Each player needs a ball and the coach uses an open area on the practice field. Cones and a precisely defined area are not needed. Players form a line facing coach.

Game: Each player has a ball and one by one hands ball to coach in the center of practice area. Coach simply tosses or kicks ball approximately 10 to 15 yards away into random areas. Players retrieve ball chasing it down, stopping it, and dribbling back to the coach or line. Don't worry the "line" will disappear almost immediately as the players start chasing their ball.

Coaching Points: Keep the players moving fast here. In the beginning and with very inexperienced players you could have the players chase the ball and pick it up with hands and return it to you as quickly as possible just to introduce the movement to the players. Then, introduce the stopping and dribbling skills. Focus on keeping the ball close as the player needs to control it more but allow for more distance between player and ball in the open field after the player first retrieves it.

Adjustments: You can throw/kick the ball farther for the more accomplished players and shorter for the less experienced players as needed. Later, you can set up gates and require the players to dribble through 1 or 2 gates before they return to you (See Diag. 1A below). Finally, the coach can move around after she throws the ball to require the players to look up and find her before they dribble back.

Chase with Gates

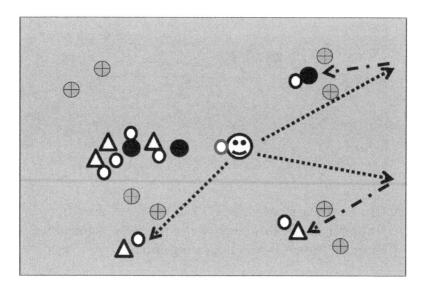

[End Diagram 10A]

Activities for Dribbling:
Toe Touches/Foundations (Warm-up)

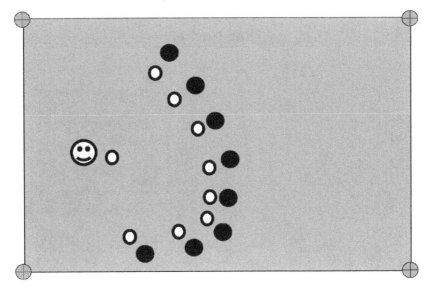

Set Up: Find an open area of your practice field and make sure each player has a ball along with you the coach – to demonstrate. Have the players with their ball facing you in a line or semi-circle.

Game: This warm-up activity could be performed at every practice. "Toe Touches" are where the player leaves the ball in front of her on the ground and lightly touches the top of it with the bottom of her toe in alternate foot fashion. The ball should barely move if at all. The coach starts the players by command and allows the player to touch the ball as many times as possible in a 15 to 20-second period. "Foundations" are where the player places the ball between his feet and, upon the coach's command, simply moves the ball back and forth from right foot to left foot using the inside of the foot – really the side/arch of the foot, as the contact point. Again, this is for 15 to 20-second time periods and the players should count repetitions and compete for the highest number.

Coaching Points: These activities teach soft touch and control of the ball at an early age which is an essential skill for all players. Do two sets of each then move on to your next activity. With the foundations, make sure the players bend their knees and do not try this activity with straight legs.

Adjustments: Longer time periods of up to 30 seconds as the players get older and stronger.

Line Soccer

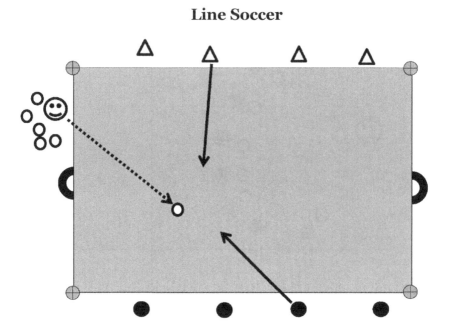

Set Up: Cone off a 15 x 20 yard grid and place small goals at each end. Divide the players into two teams and use colored pinnies to separate the teams. The team members should be assigned an individual number 1 – 4 or 5 (depending on your numbers) by the coach. Thus, two teams of four should be numbered 1 through 4 each. Line the players up for each team on opposite side lines so that #1 is facing #4 on the opposite team, #2 is facing #3, etc. Coach should have all the balls at his feet. Assign a goal for each team to attack.

Game: The coach calls out a number, such as #2 and serves a ball with a push pass into the middle of the field (see above). The two players assigned #2 should enter the field immediately upon hearing their number called, fight to win the ball, and try to dribble to their assigned goal to take a shot. The player that does not win the ball must defend his goal and try to win the ball or at least prevent a goal from being scored. If the ball goes out of bounds or past the goal, that session is over, players return to their starting points and a new number is called out.

Coaching Points: Encourage quick movements to the ball to win it or to close down defensively. Let the players be creative in dribbling to score a goal – they will figure out what works and what does not work. (If numbers are uneven, or to change the match ups, simply call out a specific number for each team – like "red 4 and yellow 5"). Try to match up evenly skilled players.

Adjustments: Eventually, call out two numbers and allow 2 v. 2 sessions to occur and even three numbers for 3 v. 3.

Simon Says

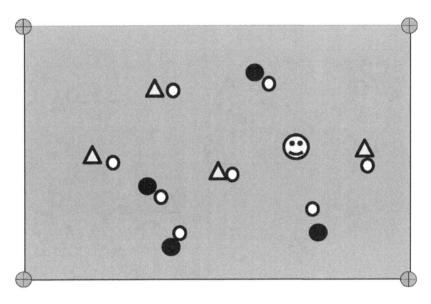

Set Up: You simply find an open area of approximately 15 x 20 yards. You may cone off or not at your choice. Each player needs a ball.

Game: Following the classic child's game of "Simon Says" the coach gives the players directions such as "Simon Says dribble". The players follow the directions. Then the coach instructs the players to stop the ball with a body part – like the foot, the elbow, even the head (for fun!). Also, instruct the kids to dribble only with their left foot, right foot, inside of feet, outside of feet, etc.

101

Don't forget the "game" portion of this exercise – if the coach doesn't say "Simon Says" and the players still do the task – then they have to do something funny like a front roll, or 5 jumps, or dribble around a distant cone, make an animal noise, etc. You decide.

Coaching Points: Instead of "Simon Says" you can make it "Coach (Your Name Here) Says" to better personalize the game. Work on skills that the players need to work on such as dribbling and ball control. This is a great warm-up activity.

Adjustments: Keep it simple and have fun! By altering the speed of the commands the players can be tested fairly keenly with this game.

Gate Dribbling

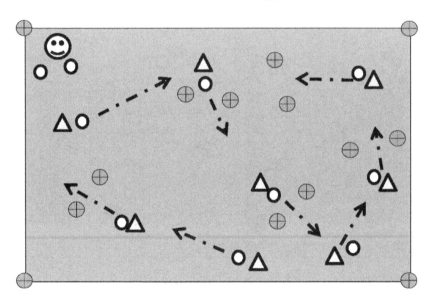

Set Up: Use a 15 x 20 yard grid. Add five or six cone gates (two cones about two yards apart) within the grid. Each player should have a ball.

Game: Upon the coach's command, players start dribbling inside the grid and try to dribble through as many gates as possible within the time period set by the coach of 1 to 3 minutes (based on age and ability). Players may not dribble through the same gate twice in a row.

Coaching Points: Encourage the players to look for an open gate and move from gate to gate as quickly as possible. Focus on the players keeping the ball close and under control. The ball may be farther from the feet when moving at speed between gates but closer to the feet when moving between the gates. Avoid allowing players to use their toes and encourage touches with the inside and outside of the feet and the laces. Teach players to keep their head up to see the activity around them.

Adjustments: Increase the time periods as the players become more confidant. Add restrictions such as only use the inside of feet, or outside of feet, left foot only. Encourage players to change speed and accelerate once through a gate until they reach the next gate, have them perform a simple "move" (e.g., step over) in between gates, etc. On your command, have them stop, then start again, do a turn, etc. as they navigate the gates.

Red Light /Green Light

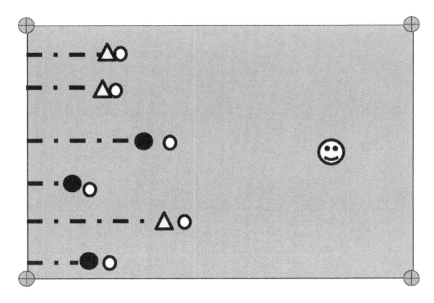

Set Up: Place corner cones in a 15 x 30 yard grid. Each player has a ball at his feet.

Game: This classic activity has been around forever. Line the players up on one endline with a ball and facing the coach. The coach yells "green light" and the players dribble straight ahead. The coach yells "red light" and the players stop immediately. The object for the players is to be the first to reach the other endline. If a player does not stop immediately when the coach yells "red light" then the coach should require such player to take three steps backwards.

Coaching Points: Focus on close control of the ball and using the inside of the foot and laces. As players develop add the outside of the feet as a contact point for the dribble. Also encourage the players to use both the left and right foot to dribble not just their favorite foot.

Adjustments: As players improve require them the look up when dribbling and not simply stare at the ball at their feet. Require the players to go all the way to the opposite endline, do a turn, and return using the green/red light commands. Require the players to only use their opposite foot to dribble for one length of the field, or use only the inside of their foot, or only the outside of their foot, etc.

Crossroads

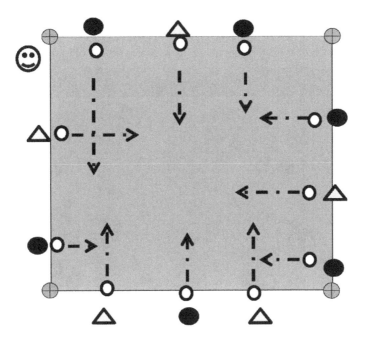

Set Up: Use a square area with corner cones approximately 12 x 12 yards. Place players on each side of the square with a ball at their feet. On your command, have the players dribble to the opposite side, turn around and dribble back to their starting point while avoiding other players.

Game: Each sideline the player touches counts as a point. Play for a minute and have the players count how many lengths they can cover before time runs out. (Each sideline counts as 1 so down and back would count as "2".)

Coaching Points: Focus on keeping the ball close with more touches when it gets busy in the middle areas and use fewer touches when more space is available. Quick turns will allow the players to earn more points.

Adjustments: Limit the players to inside of the foot only, outside of the foot only, left foot only, right foot only, etc. Direct the type of turn the player must perform – e.g., a pull back, an outside of the foot turn, a chop turn, etc. Try a larger square to give the players more room to operate in if they are struggling or if you want them to dribble for longer distance‑

Box Dribbling/Super Hero

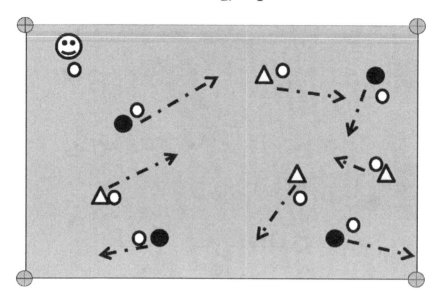

Set Up: Create a grid of approximately 15 x 25 yards. Each player with a ball at his feet. Assign each player a "super hero" (let them choose) that has a distinctive move, action, skill or pose. Let the players make up this "action" or "pose" for her super hero if it is not obvious.

Game: This simple game is a great warm-up activity too. Similar to the "Animal Farm" game already mentioned, on the coach's command to start, players simply dribble within the grid and avoid other players while finding open space. When the coach says "super hero", the players all do their super hero action, move or pose. Run for four or five times in 1 to 1.5 minute periods with a brief rest of 15-20 seconds in between.

Coaching Points: Try to focus on the players keeping the ball close and on using the proper contact surfaces – the inside, outside of the foot or laces to control the ball.

Adjustments: Add in commands such as "left foot only", or "outside of the foot only", etc. Later, add in some different commands such as "freeze" whereby they stop the ball immediately, or "stop/start" where they mus' stop the ball completely and then automatically restart the dribble, etc.

Pirates Gold

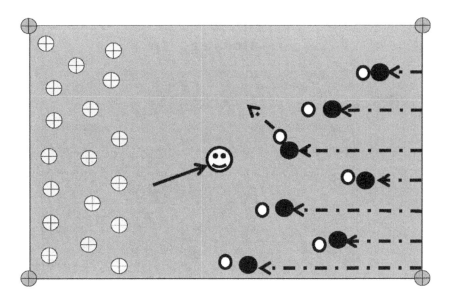

Set Up: Use corner cones to mark off a grid of approximately 15 x 20 yards. Place approximately 18 to 22 cones at one end of the grid – use yellow cones if you have them for "gold". Each player should have a ball and line up at the opposite end of the grid from the placed cones.

Game: The players try to dribble by the coach and retrieve a piece of "gold" – a free cone from the opposite side of the grid – and carry it (in their hands) to the other side of the grid from where they started. The coach should start in the middle of the grid and play passive defense against all of the dribbling players. Once the players have retrieved all the "gold" have them return the gold to its original side and "bury" it and then dribble back to the starting point.

Coaching Points: The players should dribble the ball close to their feet when under pressure or in tight places. Moves should be well timed to beat the coach as needed. In open space players should push the ball further from their feet and move faster.

Adjustments: You can have the players play in pairs and only 1 player per pair can make his dribble at a time. Add 1 or 2 defensive players to assist the coach in applying light pressure on the dribbling players. Require the players to make a move if they are skilled enough to do so.

Monster

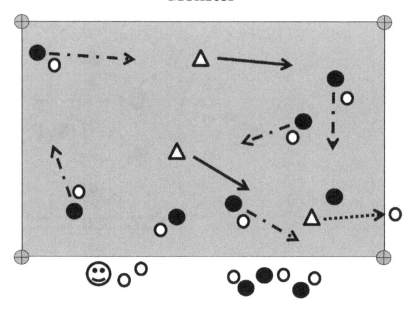

Set Up: Similar to "Knock Out" (Diagram 6), use an area of approximately 15 x 20 yards. Larger if you have more than ten players. Smaller if you have fewer than eight players. Each player has a ball.

Game: Hold one or two players out who will serve as the "monsters". Kids love to be a "monster". Other players each have a ball and are dribbling inside the grid. Upon your signal, the "monsters" enter the grid area (without their own ball) and try to kick other players' balls outside of the grid. Dribbling players try to protect their own ball. Unlike Knock Out, the dribbling players do not worry about any other ball except for their own. If your ball gets knocked out, that player must either sit out until the game is over or you can have them dribble around a distant cone, do 20 toe taps, or foundations, etc. before they can re-enter the grid and play again. If players must sit out, you can play until only a single player is left to determine the champion. Just keep the players that have been knocked out busy with a productive activity until the game is complete.

Coaching Points: Like Knock Out, this game is about dribbling in tight spaces and shielding the ball. Emphasize short quick touches of the ball and keeping your body between the attacking player and your own ball to protect it. Dribbling into "space" and away from traffic should be encouraged.

Adjustments: If your players are ready, limit their touches to only the inside of the foot or outside of the foot (harder), or left foot only for a short period of time. If the game is moving slowly, then tighten the space by moving the cones or simply walking into the grid and not allowing players to dribble outside of where you are standing.

Activities for Shooting/Kicking and Passing:

Sharpshooter

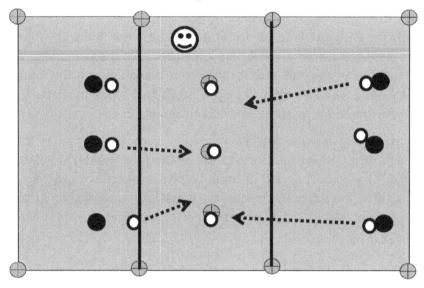

Set Up: Use a 20 x 15 yard grid. Create two end zone areas approximately 10 yards deep on each end as shown above. Place 3 to 5 flat cones in the middle of the grid with a ball balanced in the center of each cone. If more than six players then add a few more balls/cones. Divide the players into two teams and place one team in each end zone area. Each team should have three or four balls.

Game: Players try to knock a ball off of the cones in the center of the grid. The team that knocks off the most balls wins that round. The balls that miss a target in the middle should be controlled, set up, and a new shot taken by the opposing team.

Coaching Points: Focus on the accuracy of the player's kick or pass to the targeted balls on the cones. Also, encourage good control and set up of the ball by the players receiving a missed shot. You should adjust the distances according to skill and strength levels.

Adjustments: You may require the players to use the push pass technique (easier) or a full shot with the laces (harder). Require the players alternate the kicking foot once they get a feel for the game. Add a requirement that upon receipt of a ball, the player must dribble back to his endline (behind him), perform a turn and then dribble back to the edge of his end zone before he makes a pass/shot.

Whack – A – Coach

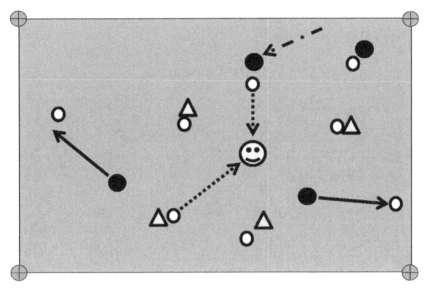

Set Up: All you need is an open area approximately 20 x 15 yards or so in size – cones are not necessary unless you want to use them to keep your players better contained. Each player needs a ball.

Game: Ask the players to start dribbling in the open area. On your signal when you say "go" or blow your whistle, the players try to hit you with their ball below your knees by kicking or "push passing" a ball at you. If they miss, the player must retrieve his own ball and try again. The coach should move around some to challenge the players. Award a point for each time a player successfully hits you with a ball below your knees. Play for 2 to 3 minutes per game and play several games.

Coaching Points: This activity has it all – dribbling, shooting, turning with the ball, and even passing if the player uses the push pass to hit you. Give positive feedback and simple instructions – like keep the ball low, keep the ball close before you shoot, etc.

Adjustments: You can add restrictions such as the shot must be taken from 3 steps away or further, only push passes for shots, only balls hit with the laces count for points – or maybe 2 points for a successful shot with the laces and 1 point for a successful push pass. Add a single defender to protect you by preventing shots if it becomes too easy to score. Become more of a moving target when you feel your players are ready for a greater challenge.

Gate Passing

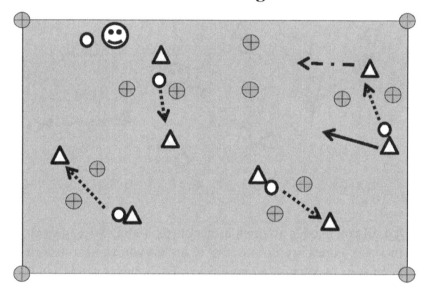

Set Up: Create a 15 x 20 yard grid. Add five or six cone gates (two cones about two yards apart) within the grid. Divide the players into pairs with 1 ball per pair.

Game: Have the players dribble the ball and pass back and forth with their partner. Upon your command have the players continue passing with their partner but now require the players to try to pass between as many different gates as possible within a 1 to 3 minute time span (based on age and ability). Players should keep count of the number of gates they pass between. Players may pass or dribble outside the gates to get into position but only the passes between the gates count toward their "score". Players may not pass between the same gate twice in a row. Team with the most passes through the gates is the winner.

Coaching Points: Encourage the players to move from gate to gate upon completion of a successful pass. Focus on the players keeping the ball on the ground and using good "push pass" technique. Make sure the kicking foot is in the shape of an "L" and non-kicking foot is pointed toward the target. Contact the middle of the ball and follow through. Also, make sure the players allow for enough space between their partner when passing – too close does not produce good passing results here or on the game field.

Adjustments: You can add an additional pass – 1 through the gates and then the receiver must control the ball and pass it right back before the players move to another gate – the "1-2 pass". Be sure you reverse the order of initial passing player after 30 seconds or so to allow both players to initiate and control the ball. Require left foot only passes through the gates.

Partner Passing

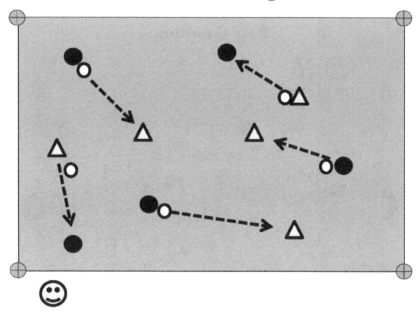

Set Up: Use an area of approximately 30 x 30 yards. Have the players find a partner with one ball between them.

Game: First, have the players push pass back and forth while standing about 6 yards apart to allow them to grasp the basic skills of push passing. Next, the players should move around the area and push pass the ball to their partner while moving. The partner should receive the ball and pass it back to the partner – all while moving around the designated area. Proceed for about two minutes and rest for a minute while you review the fundamentals of push passing with the players. This is a good warm-up activity too.

Coaching Points: Try to focus on the quality of the push pass. The pass should be on the ground and firm. Soft passes are not realistic for game conditions and do not work. Emphasize a good contact point with the inside of the foot and a good follow through.

Adjustments: Once comfortable with the basic skills of the push pass, add a combination pass where the receiving player first times the ball back to the first passer and then moves. The first passer then takes a few dribbles and delivers it again to the receiving player. After about 30 seconds, change the roles.

Pass Counting

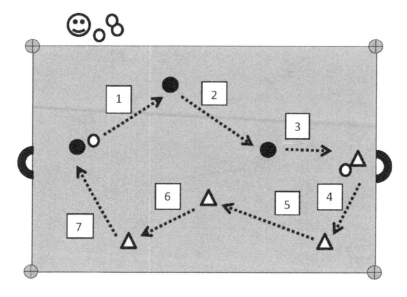

Set Up: Mark a grid of approximately 20 x 30 yards with a small goal at each end. Divide your players into two teams with separately colored pinnies. Number the players 1 – 7 (or whatever the highest number is to include all players). Spread the players out in numerical order as set forth above – add more middle-positioned players if you have more than 7 players.

Game: This game simulates game-like passing but with no pressure. Start with one ball at the foot of the #1 player near a goal. He must start the first ball and pass it to the #2 player, #2 passes to the #3 player and so on. The ball keeps rotating around. When the ball reaches the highest numbered player (#7 above) he simply passes to the #1 player and it all starts again. The players all count out loud as the ball moves around the field.

Coaching Points: Focus on good solid push passes with the inside of the foot and the ball on the ground. Receiving players should receive the ball with the inside of the foot, slightly turn, and push pass the ball to the next player. Try to have the players "side on" to the incoming ball so that he receives it, and is positioned facing slightly forward to pass it on to the next player.

Adjustments: You can add a second or even third ball (allow some space between additional balls) when the players are ready for it to keep the pace moving. If the players are ready, add restrictions such as "left foot only" or "outside of the foot only".

Tame the Dragon

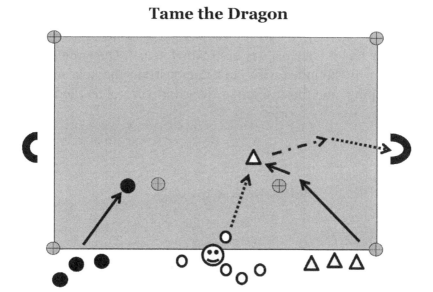

Set Up: Use a grid of approximately 20 x 30 yards with a small goal at each end behind the endline by a yard or two. Create two playing areas. Place a cone on each end that is approximately 8 yards from the endline and 8 yards from the side line (see diagram). Divide your players into two groups. Coach is on sideline at midfield with all available balls at her feet.

Game: The two groups of players line up near the corner cone at their end of the field. The coach directs the first player from a group to run inside of the cone on the field, cut and turn toward midfield and face the coach. The ball should be described as a wild dragon that must be tamed. The coach then will serve a push pass to the player's feet. The player receives the ball, turns and dribbles it toward his goal and finishes into the open small goal with a good push pass from three or five yards away. Player collects ball and returns it to the coach. The coach instructs the first player in each group not to start his run until the coach has served the pass to the other team. Coach will then alternate services to each side.

Coaching Points: Focus on the players receiving the ball under control and moving toward the goal. Demonstrate receiving the ball softly with the inside of the foot in the beginning. This game has all elements of control, dribbling and shooting – but the focus here is control and quick change of direction.

Adjustments: The coach can vary the services from an easy push pass (on the ground), to a firm push pass, to a bouncing ball, and even an air ball if your players are ready for that. Once the ball starts to get air bound, revisit and demonstrate the sole of the foot "trapping" and the cushion or "elevator" control methods.

Activities for Defending:

Line Soccer

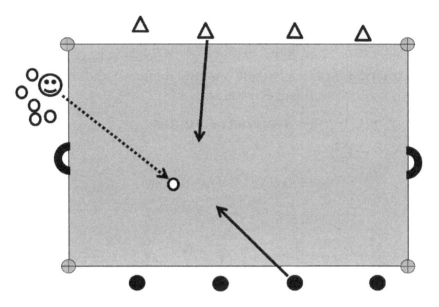

Set Up: Cone off a 15 x 20 yard grid and place small goals at each end. Divide the players into two teams and use colored pinnies to separate the teams. The team members should be assigned an individual number 1 – 4 or 5 (depending on your numbers) by the coach. Thus, two teams of four should be numbered 1 through 4 each. Line the players up for each team on opposite side lines so that #1 is facing #4 on the opposite team, #2 is facing #3, etc. Coach should have all the balls at his feet. Assign a goal for each team to attack.

Game: The coach calls out a number, such as #2 and serves a ball with a push pass into the middle of the field (see above). The two players assigned #2 should enter the field immediately upon hearing their number called, fight to win the ball, and try to dribble to their assigned goal to take a shot. The player that does not win the ball must defend his goal and try to win the ball or at least prevent a goal from being scored. If the ball goes out of bounds or past the goal, that session is over, players return to their starting points and a new number is called out.

Coaching Points: Encourage quick movements to the ball to win it or to close down defensively. Let the players be creative in dribbling to score a goal – they will figure out what works and what does not work. (If numbers are uneven, or to change the match ups, simply call out a specific number for each team – like "red 4 and yellow 5"). Try to match up evenly skilled players.

Adjustments: Eventually, call out two numbers and allow 2 v. 2 sessions to occur and even three numbers for 3 v. 3.

Defensive Angles

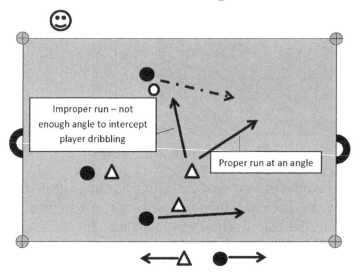

Banana Run - Defense 1 v. 1

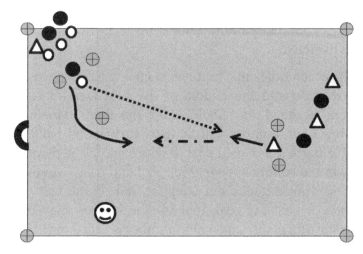

Set Up: Use a grid of approximately 20 x 25 yards with a small goal at one end. Place two cones (offensive) in the center about 20 yards from the small goal, another two cones (defensive) about 5 yards inside the endline and 5 yards inside the sideline, and, finally, a third cone (angle cone) about 5 yards from the defensive cone at an angle and slightly closer to the offensive cone – see above diagram for details.

Game: Arrange the players (no pinnies needed) with half behind the offensive cones and half behind the defensive cones facing the center of the field. The defensive player starts with the ball and serves it with a firm push pass to the feet of the first offensive player in line. The offensive player receives the ball, controls it, and immediately attacks the goal and tries to score. The defending player must run around the angle cone (far side) before she can defend the attacking player. Players alternate lines after each turn.

Coaching Points: No long shots but encourage the players to receive, control, dribble and then shoot with a firm push pass to score. The attacking player must dribble past the defending player in order to score. The defending player's run around the angle cone is sometimes called an "angled run" or you might just call it a "banana run" for fun because of its curved nature. The idea here is to teach players how to better position themselves when running to "close down" an attacking dribbler – encourage the defender to move quickly toward the ball in this manner.

Adjustments: Change sides from where the defenders start their runs from time to time (make sure you adjust the angle cone when you do). This game is good for attackers too – have them try "moves" and make sure they control the ball first before they start to dribble. If you have more than 10 players you can set this game up in both directions (using two separate goals) to avoid lines and waiting.

Activities for Ball Control:

Circle Pass

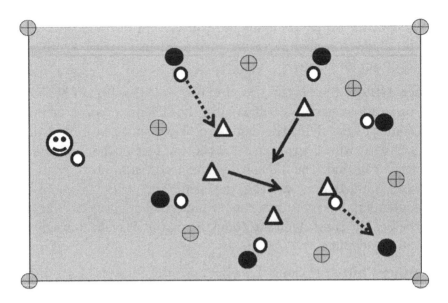

Set Up: Create a circular area using five or six cones with a diameter of approximately 15 yards. Divide your team into two even teams of four to six players. If you have more than 12 total players you may need to enlarge the circle by a few yards. Place one team on the outside in a circular shape in between the cones. Each outside player should have a ball at his feet. Place the other players inside the circle without a ball.

Game: The players on the inside simply move toward an open outside player who serves the inside player a good push pass on the ground. The inside player receives the ball, controls it, and push passes it back to the same outside player. After passing back, the inside player then runs to another outside player to receive another pass and repeats. Inside players should move quickly from open outside player to player. Run for one to two minute time periods and then change the inside and outside players.

Coaching Points: This simple activity allows for many touches and repetitions on both push passes and controlling a moving ball. Focus the players on either a "soft touch" cushion control or a "trap" with the sole of the foot on top of the ball. On the push passes, concentrate on keeping the ball on the ground with the proper contact point using the middle of the inside of the foot on the middle of the ball.

Adjustments: You may require only push passes with the left foot or right foot. Control by a cushion only or by the sole of the foot only. After the players get a feel for this first phase, have the receiving player take the ball and turn it, dribble to another player, and then push pass it to a new, open outside player. The outside player will then serve it back to the inside player who will then receive it and move to yet another player.

Circle Ball Control – Air

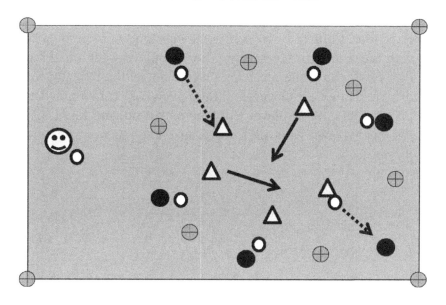

Set Up: Cone off a circular area using five or six cones with a diameter of approximately 15 yards. Divide your team into two even teams of four to six players. If you have more than 12 total players you may need to enlarge the circle by a few yards. Place one team on the outside in a circular shape in between the cones. Each outside player should have a ball in his hands. Place the other players inside the circle without a ball.

Game: The players on the inside simply move toward an open outside player who serves the inside player an underhanded tossed ball.

The inside player receives the ball, controls it, and push passes it back to the same outside player. After passing back, the inside player then runs to another outside player to receive another tossed ball and repeats. Inside players should move quickly from open outside player to player. Run for one to two minute time periods then change inside and outside players.

Coaching Points: This simple activity allows for many touches and repetitions on both controlling an air ball and push passing it. Focus the players on either a "soft touch" cushion control or a "trap" with the sole of the foot on top of the ball. On the push passes, concentrate on keeping the ball on the ground with the proper contact point using the middle of the inside of the foot on the middle of the ball.

Adjustments: You may require only push passes with the left foot or right foot. Control by a "soft touch" cushion only or by a "trap" with the sole of the foot only. After the players get a feel for this first phase, have the receiving player control the ball and turn it, dribble to another player, and then push pass it to a new outside player. The outside player will then pick it up, and toss it back to the inside player who will then receive it and move to yet another player.

Other Activities for General Playing / Scrimmages:

Small Sided, 2 v. 2, 3 v. 3, etc.

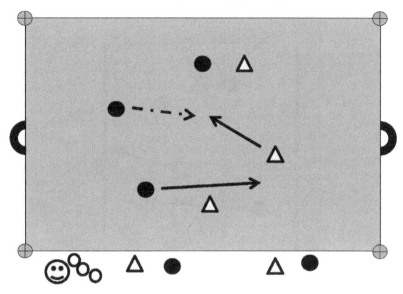

Set Up: Cone off a grid of approximately 15 x 20 yards with a small goal at each end. Divide your players into two teams with separately colored pinnies.

Game: This is basically a small-sided scrimmage where you can play 2 v. 2 or 3 v. 3 or 4 v. 4 depending on the numbers you have on your team or at practice that day. Simply let them play to score a goal as assigned. The coach should have a supply of balls and roll them in as needed. You can rotate in new players every minute or two to keep them fresh but without too much sideline sitting.

Coaching Points: Try to focus on only one or two points that you covered earlier in your practice session such as close dribbling, ball control or defensive positioning and see how the players are using a new skill or if they have learned it properly. Do not over coach here – let them play!

Adjustments: You may have a neutral player that is always offense and trying to score. Indicate that player with a third colored pinnie. So you play 2 v. 2 (red v. blue) with a third player (yellow) that is always on offense. Require that at least two players must touch the ball before the team can score – but do not over coach this as simply dribbling straight to goal is a great asset at this age!

Free Play/Small Sided – End Zones

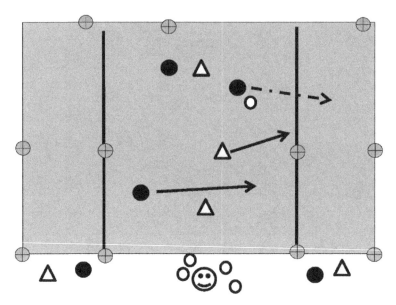

Set Up: Cone off a grid of approximately 20 x 30 yards with an "end zone" of approximately 4 yards deep at each end. Divide your players into two teams with separately colored pinnies.

Game: This is basically a small-sided scrimmage where you can play 2 v. 2 or 3 v. 3 or 4 v. 4 depending on the numbers you have on your team or at practice that day. Simply let them play to score a "touchdown" in the assigned end zone by dribbling or passing into the end zone with the ball under control. The coach should have a supply of balls and roll them in as needed. You can rotate in new players every minute or two to keep them fresh but without too much sideline sitting. You can start by requiring players to dribble into the end zone and stop the ball under control for a touchdown.

Coaching Points: Ball must be possessed and under control in the end zone to score. This works as a "free play" activity with the larger number of players involved. Try to focus on only one or two points that you covered earlier in your practice session such as close dribbling, ball control, or defensive positioning and see how the players are using a new skill or if they have learned it properly. Do not over coach here – let them play!

Adjustments: After dribbling into the end zone for points you can add that a player may pass to a teammate in the end zone where his teammate must control the ball in the end zone for a point. Again, add a neutral player that is always offense and trying to score. Indicate that player with a third colored pinnie. So you play 2 v. 2 (red v. blue) with a third player (yellow) that is always on offense. Require that at least two players must touch the ball before the team can score – but do not over coach this as simply dribbling/passing straight to goal is a great asset at this age.

4 v. 4 Game/Scrimmage

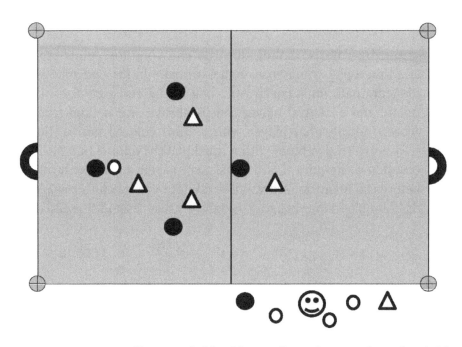

Set Up: Use a small game field with small goals at each end. Divide the players into two teams of four or five each. Put them in different colored pinnies.

Game: Let them play a "game" and try to score goals. Either play all your players or substitute as needed if players get too tired. Use a "neutral" player who is always offense if numbers are uneven.

Coaching Points: Really, just let them play. Encourage all players to get involved and do not worry about "left" and "right" side assignments – just let them find the ball and respond accordingly when possession changes from your team to the other team.

Chapter 7

GAME DAYS

So, you have organized your team, held several well-planned practice sessions, and communicated actively with the parents of your players. It is now time for your first game or scrimmage against another team. Different soccer organizations conduct games or scrimmages in various manners at the U6 and U8 levels.

Usually the weekend events for the U6 age group will consist of 3 v. 3 or 4 v. 4 "games" to small goals on fields measuring approximately 30 x 20 yards. The U8 group will usually play on a slightly larger field and sometimes with larger goals too. Scores and wins/losses are not kept and typically there are no referees. If there are not referees, then the coaches are allowed onto the field to direct their players and coordinate the re-starts when the ball goes out of bounds. Most out of bounds for both endlines and sidelines use a restart of the game, usually with a kick, from the place on the line where it went out.

Check with your league's local practices to determine the rules. Some leagues may actually use "throw –ins" to restart a ball from the sideline when it goes out of bounds, as is required by the standard rules of soccer used by older age groups. See the definitions section for throw-in details.

As far as the "games" go, the first thing to remember is that the results of the event and score do not matter. What matters is that your players are learning soccer skills and they are interested and excited about playing soccer. Most important is that they are having fun!

Now some of you that are more sports minded may be saying, "What is the point of introducing kids to sports if you do not care about 'winning'"? That is a fair question and the answer is really simple. Does it really matter who wins a U6/U8 soccer game? Are the results of U6/U8 games going to determine the actual future success of any player? Does winning or losing at this age really measure the skill level of an individual player? The answer to all of these questions is "no."

These young players will look to you and your attitude about the weekend "game" or scrimmage. **Pro Tip 20:** If you place too much emphasis on winning and not on learning then the players will do the same thing. They will skip vital steps in the development of soccer skills.

For instance, if winning — not learning — is the only objective then your young players might start kicking the ball toward the empty goal with their toes whenever they are in possession. While they might win a few more games early on, by the end of the season another team that has learned to dribble, play a bit of defense, and to kick a ball properly will outplay the toe-balling early season winning team every time there is a match between the two.

Just watch and see – it happens every season in virtually every league. You want to be the coach of the team that is learning the basics and not worried about results or game scores. By the end of the season, you will have a better trained team. Sometimes it takes a season or two to catch up but your team will excel if it sticks to the basics contained in this book.

PRE-GAME WARM-UP

Get your players organized and do some warm-up activities (see Chapter 6) 20 to 30 minutes before a game starts. This helps you check if all of them are present and are mentally and physically ready to play. If you do not have access to a game field for the warm-up, do not worry. A small area of grass off the game field will do.

You only need about 10 to 15 minutes to get the players physically ready. The rest of the time will be spent talking to them about the game, checking their uniform and water supply (did they bring water?), and figuring out how to play and substitute them during the game. Also, you might want to give instructions to them such as "You will stay near me on the sideline before the game;" "You will stay or sit on the blanket (or bench if available) when you are not playing;" "Always keep your socks pulled up and over your shin guards;" etc.

Whether you have access to a game field or just a small area of grass to warm-up in, you should play a game or conduct an activity or two to get your players ready for the game or scrimmage. A couple of these activities might be the training sessions from Chapter 6 under Dribbling or Kicking/Shooting. For example, review **Diagrams 21** (1 v. 1 **and 26** (Partner Passing) as good pre-game warm-ups.

BENCH CONTROL

I mentioned earlier in Chapter 3 that you should have in your equipment bag either a portable, collapsible bench or a large water-resistant blanket - the type you might use at a picnic. The idea is to have a defined area for your players to sit when they are not on the field during the game.

The idea of not standing by their parents may be a problem with some non-playing fidgety kids. So if you can give them a defined area on the sideline to stand, or better yet, to sit in, it will make your life much easier during the game. Ask your assistant coach, if you have one, to corral the players responsibly into the area while you focus on coaching and organizing those on the field.

Before the game starts, I strongly recommend that you have all the kids bring their water bottles over to the bench/blanket area and not leave those bottles with their parents watching the game from a different location on the field. As in school and during other activities, kids are separated from their parents and they will be in this case too. Except in emergencies, do not allow non-playing players to go to their parents and sit or chat with them until the entire game is completed.

During halftime, you will find that the portable bench or blanket is a great place for the kids to sit on and drink some water while you talk to them about the game or scrimmage. With the game finished, you should clean up the place you are occupying and vacate it for the warm-up activities of another team scheduled for a next game, if any. This is just basic courtesy.

RULES OF THE GAME

The Rules of the Game are pretty basic but you should consult with your association and make sure that you review the rules specifically adopted for this age group. Soccer is governed by a large worldwide governing body known as FIFA ("Federation Internationale de Football Association") which publishes "The Laws of the Game." This publication is the official international standard for the rules of soccer.

Most countries, however, have their own national organizations that work with and through FIFA to provide a universal approach to the rules of soccer, such as the USSF ("United States Soccer Federation") which governs most of the United States rule-making organizations and, in England, the FA ("Football Association"). These and other national soccer organizations may alter the FIFA rules in non-international events to better suit the needs of their domestic leagues and in many youth, high school and college leagues.

This information is simply provided to give you a frame of reference. You do not need to worry too much about these official rules and some of the variances at this age. **Pro Tip 21:** Early in your coaching career, purchase or borrow a copy of the FIFA Laws of the Game and study them. It will help your understanding of the game especially at older age levels and when you are watching a professional match either live or on television.

You should know your league's basic rules so that you can convey them to your players and parents. In general, most leagues at this age level will play in either a 3 v. 3 or 4 v. 4 format. There will not be a goalkeeper nor will there be "offsides" to worry about. This means the players on the field can go anywhere at any time. Almost all leagues will use small portable goals.

Diagram 27 – Game Field

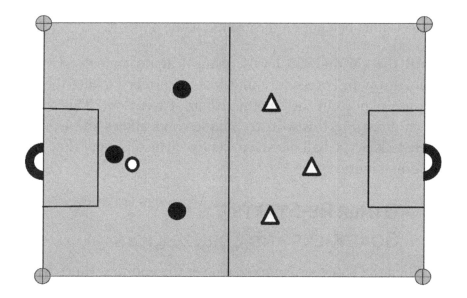

Some leagues will provide a small semicircle or box in front of the small goal to prohibit any players from entering this area. The purpose of this rule is to disallow standing in front of the small goal to prevent opponents from scoring. It is a good practice.

THROW-INS

A couple of basics for those new to the sport. A "throw-in" (for older age groups) occurs when the ball crosses either sideline. First, in soccer, the ball is not out of bounds until it crosses the sideline or endline entirely. This may be frustrating for many players/parents who are used to the basketball rules that consider the ball to be "out" if it merely touches the line. But this is a soccer "thing" so just learn and bear with it! It is a universal rule in soccer.

Second, any player of the team that did not send the ball out is allowed to pick it up with his/her hands and throw it back into play. The technique is to hold the ball with both hands and take it behind the head till it touches the nape of the neck and then throw it back onto the field — preferably to one of his teammates. Both feet must be kept on the ground while doing it.

For the U6 and U8 levels, many leagues smartly skip the actual "throw-in" procedure and instead prefer kicking the ball back into play from the sideline where it went out. This avoids over-emphasizing throw-in techniques and allows the learning players to kick the ball more frequently - which is what they need to be doing more.

OTHER RE-STARTS - GOAL KICKS AND CORNER KICKS

When the ball goes *completely* over the endlines (lines where the goals are placed), the game is restarted either with a **goal**

kick if the attacking team kicked the ball out or with a **corner kick** if the defending team kicked it out.

A goal kick is taken by the defending team from within the "goal box" (small rectangular box) in front of the goal where the ball was played out of bounds by the attacking team. Sometimes there may not be a "goal box" for these age groups in which case the ball is placed somewhere in front of the goal and kicked back into play.

When your team takes a goal kick, simply place the ball a few steps in front of your own goal and have one of your players kick it toward another player on your team. Try to play the ball out wide and not down the middle. It is easier to defend that way if the ball is intercepted by the opposing team.

A corner kick is taken by the attacking team from a corner of the field (a small triangle is located in each of the four corners for this purpose). It is taken in the corner on the side of the goal where the ball went out of bounds. Again, some leagues will not allow corner kicks for these age groups and will merely restart a game with a goal kick. Many leagues, however, may use them and you should know the procedure.

If your team is taking the corner kick, have one of your players take the kick from the corner and aim for the area in front of the goal. Place the rest of your players somewhere in front of the goal you are attacking, and try to score. If your team is defending a corner kick, position your players a few steps away from their own goal and let them try to win the ball after it has been kicked; they should keep it from entering their goal. Pretty straight forward really. Again, do not over think these restarts at this age — keep them simple!

KICK OFFS

Finally, to start a game and to re-start it in the second half, a team takes a kick from the center of the field, that is, the center spot in the middle of the large circle on the field. A toss of a coin decides which team will kick the ball first to start the game and the opposite team restarts it similarly in the second half. After each goal is scored, the non-scoring team restarts the game by taking a kick from the center spot.

The basic rules require the non-kicking team to remain outside the center circle until the ball is kicked by the starting team. Only two players from the kicking team are allowed inside the circle - all others from both teams must be in their own halves. The non-kicking team should be between its own goal and the center circle to prevent a player from kicking the ball directly into the open goal from the kick-off.

It is really simple to restart a game and you will not forget once you see it; so do not worry. **Pro Tip 22:** I would recommend that you train your players at an appropriate time *not* to simply kick the ball hard toward the other goal - this will not work at older levels and it shows a certain lack of understanding of the game by the players and the coach.

Have two players stand near each other at the center spot and let one pass the ball to the other. *The kicking player can only touch the ball once before another player must touch it.* The ball should move forward and go at least slightly across the center line before the next player "gets hold of it." Then he/she can start to dribble the ball toward the goal.

FORMATIONS

Do not be overly concerned with "formations" when your U6 kids are playing 3 v. 3 or 4 v. 4. Space them out and make sure they maintain an appropriate distance between themselves. At the U8 level, however, you can introduce a semblance of a "formation" especially if you are playing 4 or more per side. Formations do not figure much into youth soccer so do not be afraid of them. This is truly one of the unnecessary worries in youth soccer - just like the characters in the *Wizard of Oz* walking through the forest chanting "Lions and tigers and bears - oh my!" Formations are virtually meaningless at this age!

I recommend that in 3 v. 3 games or scrimmages you simply let your U6 kids play and follow the ball. **Pro Tip 23:** If you have some more advanced players, let some play defensively while some can aggressively attack the goal! Switch their roles so that no single player gets stuck with only one role.

Encourage your players to steal the ball from the other team, but help the "defensive player" to protect the goal area and not sit or stand in front of the goal. Tell him/her to guard the area from a distance of 5 or 10 yards or even at midfield. On winning the ball the defensive player must move into the opposing half in a bid to score a goal. This is one way defenders can learn how to strike from the back.

The "shape" you should encourage while arranging players on the field is that of a triangle - one of soccer's favorite shapes. See diagrams below but do not worry too much if your players do not stick to it. Let the kids move as they want to and figure out what works best for them. Keep them spread out in the field by telling them: "Do not stand in your teammates' way;" or "let [other player's name] do her job" and "be in a good position to win the ball if your teammate does not".

Diagram 28 – Formations 3 v. 3

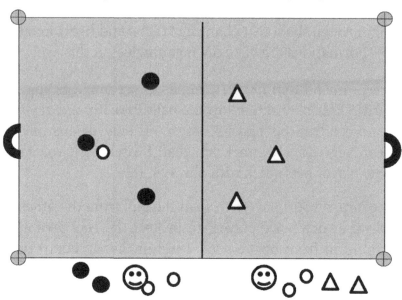

Set-up: Do not rack your brains over formations. It really is not that important for learning soccer skills at this age level. This is a basic set-up for a 3 v. 3 format on the field. You can assign one player a little more "defensive" role and let the other two find the ball. All players play offense as well as defense. One player on "defense" could have a little more responsibility closer to his goal. Rotate this responsibility among all players if you take this approach.

Coaching Points: Encourage all players to get involved and do not worry about "left" and "right" side assignments – just let them find the ball and respond accordingly when the other team is in possession of the ball. You will see the all-important "soccer shape" of a triangle in this set-up which at a higher level will give a team passing options.

Adjustments: If your players are overpowering the other team, put your goal scorer in the defense position and the weaker ones in the front so that they get some confidence in possessing and playing the ball.

If your league plays 4 v. 4 then the same approach applies to that format, too, although the basic triangle shape will change to that of a diamond - another one of soccer's favorite shapes - with one "defender" and three attackers. See below. Again, you should be focused on spacing your players out and, more importantly, allowing your players to try to retain the ball longer when they play.

Diagram 29 – Formations 4 v. 4

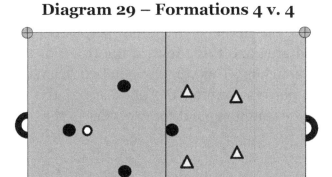

Set Up: These are two basic set ups for a 4 v. 4 format. The black team (circle) is using a diamond 1-2-1 approach with one defender and three players in midfield/forward. The three upfront try to pressure the ball while the assigned defender supports and covers the goal more but should not stand in front of the goal like a goalkeeper. All players play offense and all players play defense. One player on "defense" can have more responsibility closer to his goal. Rotate this defensive responsibility among all players. The light team (triangle) is set up in the box 2 – 2 with two players playing defense and two players playing offense. Easy to understand but sometimes it adversely impacts a player's willingness to go forward (if a "defender") or play defense (if an "attacker"). I like the 1-2-1 better for the U6/U8 age groups.

Coaching Points: Again, encourage all players to get involved and do not worry about "left" and "right" side assignments – just let them find the ball and respond accordingly when possession changes from your team to the other team. You will see the all-important "soccer shape" of a diamond in the 1-2-1 set up which at the higher levels will give a team passing options.

Adjustments: Again, if your team is overwhelming the other team, put your goal scorer in the defensive area and see if he can get the ball to a weaker player(s) on your team that might need some confidence in possessing the ball.

If your league plays in a 5 v. 5 format, which I do not recommend at this level, then simply play two players in the back/midfield area and three toward the front, or the goal that your team is attacking. This will give you two "triangles" with the back/middle players forming the apexes and the front center player being the common point for two sides to the triangles.

Diagram 30 – Formations 5 v. 5

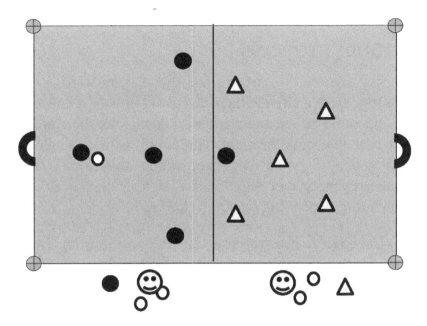

Set Up: These are two basic set ups for a 5 v. 5 format. The black team (circle) is using a diamond 1-3-1 approach with one defender, three midfielders and one forward. The three midfielders play both offense and defense while the designated defender and attacker play more committed defense and offense, respectively. The light team (triangle) is set up in the box 2-1-2 with two players playing defense, one player in the midfield, and two players playing offense. Again, easy to understand but sometimes it adversely impacts a player's willingness to go forward (if a "defender") or play defense (if an "attacker"). I like the 1-3-1 better for the U6/U8 age groups because it teaches collective offense and defense without over specializing roles at an early age.

Coaching Points: See comments for 4 v. 4 formation, above.

Remember what we talked about in Chapter 2? The focus for U6/U8 level is on ball contact, dribbling, and winning the lost ball back. Do not crush what has been taught to these players by making them stand in certain areas away from the ball waiting for a pass that may never come. If you have a bunch of ball-winning dribblers who go straight to goal, you have done a great job!

SUBSTITUTIONS

During a game, substitutes are the players waiting on the sideline to play. We already have discussed how to manage yours by making them sit on the portable benches or the waterproof blanket that you have brought. Hopefully, with the help of an assistant coach, if you have one, you will be able to keep them in one place. Every player should play at least half a game and probably more depending on your roster size.

Try to be fair in how you use your substitutions and how you decide which players "start" a game and which ones sit on the sideline. Rotate the starters for every game so that each player has an equal number of chances. The players may not care about when they play, but I guarantee you that their parents will! Also, if your league does not use quarters, then be sure to use a watch and, as it indicates the midpoint of the half, substitute your players on the field with the ones on the sideline as required.

If you play 3 v. 3 and have six players the math is pretty easy - play each player for half of each half. If you have fewer players then rotate them in such a way that each stays in longer. For instance, if you have five playing in a 3 v. 3 league match of two 16-minute halves, then two come out at the eight-minute mark and two new players go in. The third player that stayed in comes out at the twelve-minute mark and one of the original starters goes back in for the last four minutes. Then in the second half, reverse the "starting" rotation and allow the two first half substitutions to get extra minutes now.

All kids should play fairly equal time. Soccer is not all about letting your best player(s) play extra time at the expense of those who are not so skilled. While this does not help the latter, a coach should bear in mind that playing time should be divided among his players as fairly as possible.

It is not about winning and any extra time for the "best player(s)" at the expense of another player is not improving the player that was shorted some playing time. It is not always a perfect science but it usually works out in a fair manner if the coach tries to be equitable with his playing time among his players.

Some parents will time the duration of their child's playing time, so be prepared to explain your system if it does not work out perfectly during all games. **Pro Tip 24:** Mistakes will happen with playing time - just apologize and move on or fix them at the next game. Nothing like awarding a "player of the day" recognition at the end of a game/scrimmage to boost a player's (or his parents') self-esteem if his playing time was accidentally shortened.

COACH'S ATTITUDE ON GAME DAY

During your game or scrimmage, keep things simple, be positive and do not over-coach your players. Arrive early and get set up on time. Your players and their parents need a beacon of leadership and a safe haven when they arrive to the field. Remember that what you say and do at and before the game will have either a positive or a negative impact on most players and some parents for the rest of the day.

We reviewed some of the coach and player characteristics in Chapter 2. You may recall that players at this age have lots of energy and will go extremely hard for short periods of time. They are creative and will use their big muscles to jump and run better than their small muscles, and they like to be led or instructed what to do. During the "game" you must take advantage of these characteristics in a reasonable manner.

Tell your players what to do before the game starts, or pep up the one entering the game for the first time. But keep it very simple and straight forward. **Pro Tip 25:** Say things like "Try to win the ball and dribble to goal" or "If the other team gets the ball, get it back" or "If your teammates have the ball give them some room" or "Be ready to help out your teammates if they lose the ball," etc. Players will understand these simple directives better than complicated positioning or spacing tactics.

U6 kids play hard for 8 or 10 minutes while U8s last a little longer, at which point they may be pulled out and given a rest. The burst of energy displayed by them will suit your substitution plan quite well. It will also help your scrimmages.

Keep the creative element of these young players active even during games. Stoke your players' imagination while explaining vital points of the game to them. Tell them that their own goal is their "castle" and it must be protected. Describe the opponents' goal as the "dragon's den" and to keep the dragon inside they have to keep scoring goals, etc. Use whatever works for your team.

Make encouraging and complimentary comments on the individual performance of the players; these will have a positive impact on them. Do not worry too much about the team aspect. Wrap up the day with comments such as "We sure did dribble the ball well today" or "Our 1 v. 1 defensive play was awesome today," etc. These positive comments will stick in the players and their parents' minds the entire weekend.

Most important of all - have fun and make it fun for the players!

Chapter 8

IT'S ALL ABOUT THE KIDS!

CONCLUSION

At the end of the day, soccer is a game and should always be treated as one when dealing with young players. *Making Youth Soccer Fun! — Ages 4 to 8* is an attempt to give coaches of all levels a few ideas on how to make playing soccer fun while teaching the basics of the game to young players. The U6 and U8 ages are the most enjoyable times for children to learn how to play it; for coaches to teach it; and for parents to watch it. It is the coach's responsibility to insure that these years are meaningful and fun for all.

As players grow older, they need to develop their technical and tactical skills. Please check out my other books on the subject at this website, http://www.psabistonbooks.com. They could be of great help for an in-depth knowledge of the game especially at higher levels. Also, if you have any positive experiences in soccer, you can share them with me athttp://www.psabistonbooks.com.

Best of luck and see you on the field!

Below is a list of some excellent resources for soccer coaching, practice sessions, and other player development issues that you will find helpful - try your own state or local club/association's websites too:

California Youth Soccer Association - South - Coaching Resources - http://www.calsouth.com/en/coaching-ed/resources/

Florida Youth Soccer Association - Articles - http://www.fysa.com/about/coaching_articles/

Indiana Soccer (state association) - http://www.soccerindiana.org/education/coaching_lesson_plan s.aspx

NSCAA - http://www.nscaa.com/education

North Carolina State Soccer Association - Coaching Links - http://www.ncsoccer.org/lessonstraining

North Texas Soccer (association)Coaching Resources - http://www.ntxsoccer.org/coaching/fieldactivities.aspx

Ohio South Youth Soccer Association - Coaching Resources - http://www.osysa.com/coaching/coaching_articles/

Oregon Youth Soccer Association - Coaches Education - http://www.oregonyouthsoccer.org/coach_education

US Soccer - http://www.ussoccer.com/coaching-education

Paul Sabiston, a veteran soccer player and coach, has played or coached youth soccer for over 35 years at all levels. He is the author of several books — including some for soccer coaches and players alike. He resides in North Carolina with his family. Please check out his website for other great soccer books and his blog at www.psabistonbooks.com.

58195907R00086

Made in the USA
Middletown, DE
05 August 2019